TODAY'S SPIRITUALITY

The Jesus Story Revisited

TODAY'S SPIRITUALITY

The Jesus Story Revisited

Thomas R. Haney

THE THOMAS MORE PRESS

Chicago, Illinois

ISBN 0-88347-245-7

CONTENTS

THOMAS R. HANEY has been
Executive Editor of *The Catholic
Witness*, the diocesan newspaper
of Harrisburg, PA, since 1975.
He is also Secretary for Com-
munications and Publications as
well as Secretary for Adult
Spiritual Development in the
diocese. Father Haney was or-
dained in 1958, served as a pastor for ten years, taught high
school religion for fifteen years,
ten of which he served as Prin-
cipal. He has published articles in
a variety of magazines and is the
author of three previous books:
Gather Up the Fragments, *That
Nothing Be Wasted*, and *Reach
Out and Touch*.

PREFACE

GENTLENESS walks out of the mists of twilight as a shepherd with a lamb snuggled on his shoulders.

Generosity stands like huge stone jars where water has just blushed into wine in the presence of divine power.

Compassion kneels by a ditch, oblivious of its own urgencies, and bathes the wounds of a robbed and beaten traveler.

Forgiveness rushes down a hill waving sandals and a ring in the face of a son who stammers out his litany of prodigalities.

Joy spreads out on a green tablecloth of grass in a banquet of five loaves and a few fish.

Love bends down and writes on sand that will shift in the slightest breeze as if to prove how forgetful of our sins the divine Judge really is.

Peace enters a room locked against persecution and extends healing wounds to those stricken with a plague of fear.

It's the Jesus story revisited.

We enter the gospel as we would an old, familiar art gallery. We stroll around, pausing before one masterpiece and luxuriating in another.

Sometimes we enter the Jesus story bringing with us our own stories. At other times we enter the Jesus story and allow it to bring us to our stories.

Inside the Jesus story we are never alone. We bring

9

with us all those who have inspired and affirmed us. All those we have loved. All those with whom there has been a mutuality of any kind.

We place our creativity at the disposal of the Creative Spirit who guides us in the gospel through our relationships with one another as surely as lips touch in a kiss.

We dwell within the Jesus story as a lover abides in the beauty and charm of his or her beloved.

Then we emerge from the Jesus story in the hope that we can enrich others with whatever fresh insights or newly-discovered intuitions we may have experienced.

In our repeated visits to the Jesus story we discover that today's spirituality is not a way of escaping from life by huddling in the safety of the gospel verses.

Rather we recognize that today's spirituality is the fullness of life. Life lived to the fullest. Life replenished, nourished and refreshed by the living Word, dwelling among us.

In revisiting the Jesus story we come to acknowledge that today's spirituality is a journey into the stories of other people that we might share with them the life that Jesus came to give us — a life throbbing with adventure and overflowing with the hope of creative love.

THE YEAST — GOD'S GENEROSITY

LUKE 9:11-17   "... give them something
                              to eat."

Tell us about your Kingdom
    the people shouted to the man
    who would not be king
    but reigned as their storyteller.

So he cast a story over their
    fluttering attention like a net
    and soon their nostrils were filled
    with the smell of yeast exploding
sweet-tasting fresh dough into bread
    until the growling of their stomachs
began to drown out the rhythm of his words
    and the pain of their hunger
throbbed more fiercely than their ache for the
    Kingdom.

It became clear that hearts could not be filled
    with the desire for the yeast-God
    if stomachs craved bread.
The Kingdom was not to be peopled
    with disembodied spirits
    floating detached, in a distant orbit
    over and above material concerns.

Thomas R. Haney

So the storyteller would spread the tablecloth
   of his prodigality before the hungry crowd
   as he had led cripples in raucous dances
   revealed glistening sunrises to the blind
and opened deaf ears to the quivering cries of
   cleansed lepers.

Responding to the puzzled protests of his disciples
   who were more adept at calculating
   what they had left than what they had
he said, ''You yourselves give them something to
   eat,''
   while he bade five thousand to recline
   on the grassy knoll of his compassion.

Standing knee-deep in the desert of their
   bewilderment,
   his disciples gazed off
   in the direction of the sea
   brimming over with fish
   unsought, uncaught
and recalled how the storyteller had sent Peter
   to retrieve the coin of tax
   from the mouth of a fish.
How could more be demanded from those
   who had left all?

The disciples had forgotten to factor in
   the storyteller's blessing
   which summed up the Kingdom
as that which multiplies while it divides
   and adds empty baskets bulging

TODAY'S SPIRITUALITY

with the leftover recklessness
    of the yeast-God's infinite generosity.

The disciples gathered up the fragments
    of the storyteller's tales
and through their ends-of-the-earth proclamation
    made it possible for us today
    in our breaking and sharing of the bread
    to recognize the Body,
wherein bread is the bait of "fishers of men."

GOD LOOKS LIKE . . .

MARK 7:31-37   "And they brought to him a
                  man who was deaf and dumb . . ."

Lord of drums and bugles
    of bands and parades
I love the story of the deaf-mute man.

He couldn't speak
    even while stones
    cried out their "Hosannas!"
He couldn't hear
    even though demons
    shrieked and screamed
    as they plunged into Gerasene pigs.

He couldn't hear your words
    as you massaged them
    into weary souls,

13

Thomas R. Haney

"Come to me, all you who labor
   and are burdened and I will refresh you."
He couldn't approach you
   after the rich young man left
   and ask,
"What must *I* do . . .?"

So they brought him to you
   (people are good, really, aren't they?)
and you plugged his ears
   into the cosmic groan
   of human struggle,
   into the infinite hymn of human joy,
and you tickled his tongue
   until the laughter of his praise
   resounded in the vastness of your Word.

We live our lives
   in chosen silence,
   self-imposed, like earplugs.

We live our lives
   in selective silence
   like the monk who vows
   solitude between feasts
   only to avoid addressing
   the hardships of communal life.

My friend — I need to talk to him
   but I tell myself that
   timing's all-important
   so I bite my tongue and crush my words.

14

TODAY'S SPIRITUALITY

He needs me to listen
  but I chatter on
  hoping not to hear his pain
  for fear it will be my own.

Then you walk along the shores
  of my self-inflicted isolation
  where the waves crash in silence
  and the wind is mute
and you offer to blow the universe
  through my ears
  and raise my tongue
  from its suicidal tomb.

I jump at your offer
  like the leper who leapt
  out of his cancerous scales,
  like the demoniac who
  outran his devil,
  like the Lazarus who tore his shroud
  to shreds of life.

And in that moment
  you reveal to me
  what God really looks like.

He looks like
  the deaf hearing
  the dumb speaking.
He looks like the selfish finally communicating.

Thomas R. Haney

COTTON CANDY HEAVEN

LUKE 20:27-38   "Some Sadducees . . . (the ones
who claim there is no resur-
rection) . . ."

"What's heaven like?" I asked.
  "It's like cotton candy,"
  a first-grade theologian pronounced
as solemnly and seriously as any guru
    wrapped in the mystic robes
    of otherworldly wisdom.

I smiled paternally knowing full well
    that one day this little girl
    would recite the exact answer
even if "cotton candy" still made more sense to her.

Later I pondered her answer.
    Cotton candy is, after all, as soft
    as the clouds of heaven
and sweet-tasting like the milk and honey
    granted long ago as the Promised Land.

I entered, then, into the Jesus story:
    "Is heaven like one bride
    for seven brothers?"

TODAY'S SPIRITUALITY

"No. Heaven's like angels who
  rejoice when a lost sheep is found,
  when a prodigal inches home,
  when a prostitute wastes perfume
    in a bath of tearful repentance.''

"Is heaven like a childless wife?''
  "No. Heaven's like a bush that burns
  with flames that cannot consume.
Heaven's like an empty tomb where angels
  sit and sing:
    'He's no longer here!
    He's a son of resurrection!'
Heaven's like Abraham, Isaac and Jacob
  forever present to their posterity.''

I emerge from the Jesus story
  with refreshed insight.
Heaven is life.
  Heaven is joy.
    And what is, lasts.
I look at my little theologian.
  She's not far from the Kingdom.

Cotton candy after all, sticks like life
  which fades with every joyous bite
  and celebrates what is yet to come —
    the more of the everlasting Most.
Isn't it, I wondered, a lot like
  the textbook principle,
"Grace is the beginning of glory''?

Thomas R. Haney

Lord, you grant us so many rich images
  from the days of childlike wisdom
  to the moments of mature imagination,
  from cotton candy
  to angels no longer liable to death.

Anyway, heaven's where you are
  and you are with us
in our burning bushes, in our resurrections
  and, yes, even in our cotton candy.

UNWASHED HANDS

MARK 7:1-8   "Why do your disciples not
                              follow the tradition of our
                              ancestors . . .?"

Those dirty unwashed hands
  still stinking of fish
  with fingers like piranha
  tearing the roasted, unconsecrated
  lamb from its bone.

"Why don't your disciples wash?
  They know our traditions,
  more patriotic than the
Word of God."

The Pharisees who knew
  the outside of the cup so well
  couldn't know the washing

18

TODAY'S SPIRITUALITY

of baptismal tears or the
flood that trickled to death
from a side of God they'd never seen before.

Water's not just for washing.
  It's for calming when it
  churns into an arkless storm.
  It's for walking on when the sands
  of pilgrimage turn to brimstone.
  It's for changing into wine
  when earthen vessels are
  emptied of all festivity.

Water's not just for washing.
  It's for drinking when
  a woman pours her hot sins
  into the cool depths of Jacob's Well
  and slakes her immortal thirst
  with living water.

I sat by the edge of the ocean
  an edge as soft as sand-soaked water
  an edge as close as the next tide
  and as far off as the moon.

I listened to the waves shouting back and forth,
  "In the beginning was the chaos
  and the chaos was with God
  and the chaos was made order."

And I wondered if God ever got his hands dirty
  like the potter's, fashioning flesh out of clay

Thomas R. Haney

like the baker's, kneeding manna
  out of desert fiber
like the artist's, drawing sandy graphics
  of hidden, shameful sins
like the architect's, destroying and
  rebuilding temples over a holiday weekend.

And I knew he did
  as surely as there are children
  with buckets and shovels and
  sandcastles that look like
  pineapple upside-down cakes.

And I knew he'd never wash his hands of us.

THE MINSTREL

MARK 12:28-34   "Which is the first of all
                           the commandments?"

The young handsome minstrel
  sang in the square
  each evening when the mountains
  looked like spider webs
  in the rays of the setting sun.

The young handsome minstrel
  sang songs of love
  and the people weary from

20

TODAY'S SPIRITUALITY

the hair-splitting of law-keeping
and worn by the day's hot labor
would gather near the well
and listen to his songs of love.

No one knew where the minstrel lived.
It was rumored that he spent
his nights in a cave of prayer
and his days among the lilies of the field
and then at eventide he'd appear
to sing his songs of love.

The rulers of the village
were deeply disturbed
and their anger rumbled like
an echo in a tomb.

"If the people keep listening
to the minstrel's songs of love,"
they said,
"they'll know no fear
and we will lose control."

So the rulers of the people
made a law:
"There will be no singing
of songs of love in the square."

The minstrel smiled
and walked to the shore of the sea.

Thomas R. Haney

So many people came to hear him
   sing his songs of love
   that he boarded a boat
   and pushed out from the shore
   and sang his songs of love.

The rulers of the village
   were deeply disturbed.
"If the people keep listening
   to the minstrel's songs of love,
   they'll be so busy loving one another
   that they'll forget to love their God
   and we will lose our control,"
they said.

So the rulers went one night
   to the minstrel's cave of prayer
   and cut his tongue out of his head.

The minstrel was never seen again
   but the people for years after
   gathered in the square
   and sang his songs of love.

They remembered his refrain,
   "Though my tongue should die,
   my Song will live forever
like a Sigh."

TODAY'S SPIRITUALITY

THE BAKERY SHOP

JOHN 6:41-51   "This is the bread that comes
                      down from heaven . . ."

There's a bakery shop
  in the middle of the block
  that sits like a rusty can
  amid porcelain treasures.
If you slow down your busy steps
  you can smell the rich aroma
pouring out of the little man's doughy thurible.
He says, "It's Italian bread" but
  there's always a wink and a smile.
He whispers the price like words of consecration
  and delivers the loaves like communion.

Down the street there's a little church
  newly renovated
  but aged with debt.
There's a little man there too
  who's preoccupied with bread.
"It's flesh," he claims, "for the life
  of the world" and there's no
  wink, no smile, no conviction,
  no price except that sweaty debt.

And, Lord, where is your sacrament?

23

Thomas R. Haney

My faith tells me it's in your church
  but I keep going to the bakery.

Outside the bakery,
  I hear friendship calling across
  the air waves of a honking horn
and know You are here.
I see love in little eyes drawing
  a bead on a caterpillar which
  taxis confidently
  in its holding pattern
and know You are here.

I sit across from a smile whose
  laser beam of affirmation
  disintegrates my social anxiety
and know You are here —
  and I want to celebrate!

So I gather the sights, sounds and smells
  the smiles and feelings
  all the flesh of my world
  where I experience You.

I bring these gifts,
  my flesh-enlivened world
  and celebrate my experience of You
  in broken bread and living wine
  and the bakery and church are one,
the sacrament is complete.

THE WATER'S ROMANCE

JOHN 2:1-10   "The waiter in charge tasted
                      the water made wine . . ."

I loved you from
    the very first moment
    you tamed me, the water sighed,
as He gazed into earthen jugs
    at the womb of life
    that night in Cana.

You drew me from my
    wild careening
    in those chaotic days
and I in turn embraced you
    in John's river
    and touched the soft side
    of divine retribution.

Why, then does my hallowed Creator
    respond to the flesh of his flesh
    the bone of his bone
by wasting infinite power
    on so frivolous a feat?

Why does he who refused
    to raise the smell of bread
    out of innocent stones

25

now make water blush
  in his presence?

Because, the wine sang out,
  Israel and Yahweh
  have always loved
as bride and groom.

Because the crucifixion
  of disordered flesh
  must be balanced by
  the re-creation of all things new
because transfiguration
  must precede crucifixion.

Because joy must shout
  its hosannas loud
  before sorrow rolls
  the stone of death
because life is a gift
  and the gift, a surprise —
  that the wrappings of death
  cannot hold life bound.

Water into wine:
  life celebrating love
  and love binding the marriage of
the humdrum and the ecstatic
the bland and the inspired
the ordinary and the mystical.

THE PARADOX OF ZEAL

JOHN 6:60-69   ". . . many of his disciples
                      left him. . . ."

Lord,
    I am drained like
    a waterway in a rainless desert
    by the poignancy of this scene.
There you are, revealing yourself
    in the marvel of bread,
    exuberant in the excitement
    of being shared,
and many of your disciples turn away from you
    as deliberately as the religious leaders
    who had never turned to you,
and walk with you no more.

You are left standing there
    with your good news
    ignored like yesterday's headline,
    bound by the truth
    that could make them free,
    the light shoved under
    a bushel basket
because many would walk with you no more.

Lord,
    I am perplexed like a person

27

locked in a house of mirrors
by the paradox of your vision.
You never called them back
but told those who remained
to go into the whole world
and proclaim the good news.
Where does that leave my zeal?
Whom do I seek out
like a shepherd of a mere ninety-nine
and whom do I let go of
like a pilgrim shaking
the dust from his feet?

Lord, is this the paradox of zeal?
Not even waving good-bye
to those who leave
and chasing after those
who have never arrived?

Lord,
can zeal be deflated
on the sparkling spikes
of presumption like
the priest who complained
that he was saving the saved?

We can never presume that the "saved" are saved
any more than a priest can presume
that his work is in vain
until the last absolution is prayed.

TODAY'S SPIRITUALITY

Lord,
    as I watch them walk off,
    walking no longer with you,
    away from the bread that is flesh,
    your gaze falls on me
    and, though I can never presume
    that I'll always walk with you,
    I plead, "To whom shall I go?
    You have the words of eternal life
    for you are the Word sharing my flesh,
    you are the flesh shared as my bread."

A SOFT TOUCH

MARK 10:13-16   "People were bringing their
little children to him to have
him touch them . . ."

It's so important to touch
    like oceans caressing beaches
    or sunbeams curling golden fingers
    around an autumn meadow at evening time
    or young love holding hands without blush
among hard-nosed suitors of hard-headed goals.

Touching, like laying hands on little children's heads,
    should be soft and honest
    not like grasping and grabbing that clenches
    in the gnarled isolation of a selfish fist.

Thomas R. Haney

The Spirit God from starless eternity,
   knowing the importance of touching,
   came to feel what he had created
   and as man made his home
   where he could touch flesh and soil
   and tousle the hair of little children
after their mothers broke the barriers
of the disciples' newly formed bureaucracy.

He came as man to be touched by a mother's love,
   by sawdust and river waters,
   touched by a blind beggar's hand
   by the sight of a leper's cageless prison
and among friends
   touching grains of wheat in one bread
   touching grapes of the vine in one cup.

George knelt in his room
   far from the arrogance
   of all those "worldly" people
   and, in flight from the human,
   waited for his mystic fire.

Lord, how do we touch you?

Her eyes snapped with panic,
   horror, like a gaping wound
   split across her face.
   The priest had dropped the host at her feet.
"The host! The host!" she pointed
   in whispered agony.

TODAY'S SPIRITUALITY

Back home after Mass,
   after Holy Communion with her God
   she poured anger into her heart
   like cream into her coffee
   and blasted "those liberals"
   like the parish assistant
into tiny legalistic fragments.

Lord, where do we touch you?

The creator God became a man of limits
   knowing how important it is for us
   to touch him
in each person he identifies with:
   those who agree or disagree
   those who befriend
   and those who attack
in all that is sacramental, human and co-created.

Lord, help us to touch you honestly
   everywhere you are.

FLESH THAT'S REAL

MARK 8:27-30   "Who do people say
                                   that I am?"

We all know who the prince was.
   He used to be a frog.
We all recognized the beautiful

Thomas R. Haney

ballerina with the glass slippers.
She used to tramp around in the cinders.

But how could we know who the carpenter was?
   He was the Word
   before he was made flesh
   and the Word is infinite,
   invisible and unfathomable.

So when he asks us,
   "Who do you say that I am?"
What do we say?

You are the one who washes feet
   that kick up a fuss
   when there's no magic wand
   to make it all nice — and easy.

You are the one who calls us friends
   even while we're pretending to be yours
   because we can't bring ourselves
   to believe that God could so lower himself.
And, anyway, it'd be disrespectful and
   irreverent to call the ineffable God
   by such a familiar title as "friend."

You are the wind that blows newspapers
   down the street at night
   and cleans the gutters of our lives,
but we prefer more sacrosanct titles
   like Spirit and Word —
   it's more seemly, more respectful

TODAY'S SPIRITUALITY

than wind and newspapers
and we feel more devout.

You are the storyteller who tells a tale
   about a woman who bangs
   on the judge's door at night
   seeking retribution
and then turns our world upside down
   by jolting us into the realization
   that God is the woman seeking justice
   and we are the sleepy judge
   who doesn't want to be disturbed.

We continue to recite our creed
   professing that you are
   God made man
   but when we're pressured
   we call you God.

You are the felt presence
   when frogs leap into handsome princes
   when a chargirl glistens
   like a fairy princess
when sinners are transformed into saints.

You are the one who announces
   in an infinite pulse of intimacy
   that your home is human life —
". . . we'll come and make our dwelling in you."

Why, then, do we keep pushing you away —
   enthroning you like some

primitive idol?
Is it because the God you reveal
  is too familiar to be taken seriously,
  too hard to endure?
Is it because we prefer our version of religion
  even if it isn't yours?

LOWERING OUR BUCKETS

JOHN 4:5-42   "Give me to drink."

There is a woman coming to the well
  her bucket filled with her past
looking for water that cannot cleanse
searching for nothing but her daily routine
    when a man with a thirst
    as dry as sawdust
    as deep as prophecy
    as desperate as zeal
    as long as the road from
    Jerusalem to Jericho
approaches her with a request that echoes
  deep in the wells of human hearts,
    "I thirst."

He who separated sky from sea
  in primordial moments
  of creative providence
  waits for the woman's efforts
  to water the Vine.

TODAY'S SPIRITUALITY

So too now he who invites,
   "Come to me all you who thirst,"
   waits upon our efforts
   to offer an everyday cup of water
   given in his name
   to anyone — even the least —
in need of his refreshment.

Too often are there those who want
   God to do it all,
to heal the brokenness of our hammering hostility
   to feed those who starve
at the end of the long lines of our indifference
   to make peace flourish
   out of the ashes of bombs dropped
in rationalized aggression.

And those who would have God
   do it all without their efforts
   are pleased to preach their fervor
   "Accept the Lord as your personal Savior"
   and sing in blissful disregard,
   "Praise the Lord."

Those who would have God do it all
   swallow the living water
   into souls bloated with the joyous
   selfishness of private salvation.

Those who would have God do it all
   will never understand the urgency
   of lowering their buckets

in the presence of the One who pleads
through the parched millions
down through all ages,
  "I thirst."

THE COUNTRY CLUB

JOHN 6:4-13   "Where shall we buy bread
                               for these people to eat?"

I push against the upright pew
    hoping to straighten out my soul
    twisted with its schizophrenic
    hope of a holier, more comfortable life.

I hear the story.
It's like deja vu.
The clock of scripture seems always
    stopped at the same numbers.
Jesus feeds over 5,000 people.
I try to perk up,
    "Why did he do it?"
I mean it sounds like grandstanding.
Still it's a wonderful miracle
    and we could feel the compassion
    of the lily God, the Lord of the harvest.

Jesus may have emptied himself,
    not clinging to divine prerogatives
    but his creator power snapped
    like lightning from his blessing hands.

TODAY'S SPIRITUALITY

Of course, this miracle (we all know)
   was a prelude to the bread
   whose substance slips away
   on the echo of consecrating words
and feeds souls while bodies starve.

I sit at the club
   gazing out at the 18th green
   sipping a neighborly margarita
   waiting for my closest acquaintances.

What can I do about the 80 percent
   of the world's population who go
   to bed hungry every night?
Or the 10,000 people who'll starve
   to death in the next 24 hours?
What is that priest eating — the one
   who told us this stuff this morning
   about the grain used for U.S. cocktails
   being enough to feed a half million
   people for one year?

He has made friends with mammon,
   tired of helping the dead bury their dead?
His eyes still squinting the future
   into even larger fantasies
   his hands no longer on the plough?

His words today, a gasp of laid-back zeal?
Words that begged for help only to make us
   feel all the more helpless.

Thomas R. Haney

What can any of us do about the 80,000
  whom malnutrition will butcher
  in each day?

After all we're just blessed here at the club.
How do I know why God blessed me?
  I'll think of something.
  I'll do something.
I really do care.
  "Another margarita, please."

A FIXED DIRECTION

MATT. 16:21-27   "Peter took him aside and
began to remonstrate with
him."

In Jerusalem I will suffer
  foretold the man who wouldn't
  tell who could sit on his right or left.
Someone has to flank your glory
  said his followers who had left
  all things and wanted a return.

In Jerusalem my suffering
  will end in death
  insisted the man who
  chased foxes out of their dens.
Tell us who among us is the greatest
  countered his followers whose
  fantasies imaged kingdoms.

TODAY'S SPIRITUALITY

The Kingdom will come
  when I am lifted up
  promised the man who had
  spent his life fashioning wood.

You'll slip through this
  argued Peter who had spent
  his life entangled in nets.

Get out of my sight, you Satan!
  shouted the man of the
  desert temptations.
Once you put your hand to the plough
  there is no looking back.

Remember, said the man whose
  measuring standard was
  a widow's mite,
that a seed has to fall into the ground
  and die
so that the Kingdom may branch out.

        * * *   * * *   * * *

"Aren't we diverting the true purpose
  of our church," the man in the audience
  asked, "by all this emphasis
  on the social aspect of the gospel?
Isn't it time we began to teach virtue again?"

"We are no more diverting the mission of the
  church,"

the speaker responded,
"than Jesus was diverted from his Passion.
As for virtue, isn't justice a virtue?"

The man in the audience wasn't convinced
  any more than was Peter who
  in the end persisted in his protests
  against his Master's sufferings
  by trying to cut through them
with the cold edge of a sword.

SMALL EFFORTS COUNT

JOHN 6:1-15   "Gather up the crusts. . . ."

Lord,
  it comes as no surprise
  to us, dulled by advances
  in the commonplace wonders
  of technological commerce,
  that you who scattered stars
  into dancing galaxies by the billions
  could break a few loaves of bread
  into a banquet for thousands
  with twelve baskets of fragments
  to fill the void left by greed.

Lord, dwelling in our depths,
  there are a lot of people,
  wonderful, solid, inconspicuous

people, who respond to your call
by going around gathering up
the fragments.

Lord,
    these are the people who,
    like the bread you blessed,
    multiply their goodness
    as they divide their efforts.

They are the people
    who plant the mustard seeds
    who fill the water jars at wedding feasts
    who row the boat through storms
    who bring little children to a blessing
    who smile and step aside
    for those who need front places
    who stand at the edge of the crowd
    and weep on the way of crucifixion.

Lord,
    there are so many people
    all around us who,
    with no fanfare in the marketplace,
    care and share
    in unmedaled ways.
Help us to appreciate their presence.
    Help us to stop judging.

Lord, indwelling God,
    these are the people
    hidden in the shadow of your light

who are neither the movers nor shakers
of the world
and yet are the dreamers of dreams,
the music makers
who sing your glory in the fragments of bread.

Lord,
we thank you for these people
whose efforts in many small ways
reach to the stars
in universal concern.

YAWNING OMISSIONS

LUKE 7:36-50   ". . . she stood behind him
                      at his feet weeping . . ."

When Mary burst upon the dinner party
like a wild storm of repentance
the host evoked his austere
fidelity to petty legalism
with a partyless question of judgmental reprimand,
"Wouldn't a true prophet know
what kind of woman it is who touches him?"

And Judas who remained untouched
by a seventy-times-seven times forgiveness
covered the theft of his anxious grabbing
with a question that mimicked compassion
and mocked the news that all are forgivable,

TODAY'S SPIRITUALITY

"Why waste this ointment when its market price
   could strip the rags of poverty
   from those who should be wearing
the robes of sons and feasting on fatted calf?"

Now which do we identify with?
   The woman of fragrant penitence?
   The host of gangrenous jealousy?
   The disciple of vested greed?
   Or perhaps all of the above?

How much ointment will be lavished
   by a penitent secretly hoarding righteousness
complacently calculating sin in familiar equations
   of acts committed?

How many tears will be poured out
   on feet that trampled highways and byways
   in search of lost sheep and priceless pearls
when sins of omission are neglected in a wayside
ditch
   that we may hurry by
to neat and tidy rituals of measurable worship?

   Which debt do we claim?
The larger one trumpeting our glorious repentance
   or the smaller reflecting our humble halo?

   Can we march to the front of the Temple
when back home we are building
   bigger and better barns?

Thomas R. Haney

Can we be truly repentant
when we number among our sins of omission
those who are put and kept down
that we might climb higher?
Those who are forced to be last
that we might push our way into front places?

Those who are made to suffer destitution
that we might enjoy more luxuries?
The poor who are sprinkled with this world's
resources
that we might bathe in needless wealth?
Those of the Third World brutally enslaved
to maintain the free enterprise of First World
economics?

When we admit
"Bless me, Father, for I have sinned . . ."
does our repentance include
a lifestyle that may omit all
but a yawn at the subhuman
conditions of those for whom we pray,
"Whatsoever you do for one of these, the
least . . ."?

TODAY'S SPIRITUALITY

OUR KINGDOM COME

MATT. 27:11-14   "Are you the king of
                                  the Jews?"

If the kingdom is yeast
    thrust into dough,
    is the king a famished
    baker who squanders
    the sweet-smelling bread
    among those who can repay nothing?

If the kingdom is a mustard seed
    that bursts into a huge bush,
    is the king an exhausted
    farmer who extends the
    bounds of its protective shade
    for those who bear the heat of day?

If the kingdom is boat people
    seeking sumptuous shores
    of freedom and security,
    is the king the navigator
    steering sure through
    chaotic waters?

If the kingdom is a nation
    of starving people
    being fed from the

Thomas R. Haney

bulging silos of the
First World,
is the king the pilot who
lands the planes of plenty?

Lord, what kind of king are you?
    Instead of a throne room
    with courtiers kowtowing,
    you chose a dining hall
where you knelt and washed the feet
    of those who called you Master.

If that's the kind of king you are,
    what does that say about us?
That is really the burning issue, isn't it?
    Our position.
    Our power.
    Our prestige.
A king who has nowhere to lay his head
    who parades on a donkey's back
    who wears a crown made of thorns
    is our judgment, isn't he?

This is the judgment that splits us,
    isn't it?
If this is what our king is like,
    what must be said of
    our kingdom?
    Our loyalties?
    Our goals?
    Our ambitions?

TODAY'S SPIRITUALITY

Lord, couldn't you have been
a different kind of king?
One made in our own image and likeness?
One who could fit royally
into our version of your kingdom?

A BOUNDLESS THIRST

JOHN 4:5-42   "Give me a drink."

It was thirst that called forth
the chaotic waters and
gave life and order.

It was thirst that split a rock
in the desert journey and
refreshed with freedom.

It was thirst that plunged
into a well of grace and
splashed absolution on
a woman who had no husband
but snuggled with sin on dry nights.

No banquet here or perfumed feet
only "food to eat of which
you do not know,"
a meat as fresh as his Father's will.

Thomas R. Haney

It was thirst that drove him
  through the desert of sinful wants
  through the waters of repentance
  through the crowded streets of need
to the drywood of passion where
  the cry dredged from his arid soul
  could only have been,
"I thirst."

When we are thirsty
  we drink a glass of water
  (or in the summer a can of beer).
It's routine. Instant gratification.
  No time allowed to delay satisfaction
  and feel desire as passion.

Sometimes we're so busy,
  so industrious, so compulsive
  slaking our thirst
for success or comfort or security or power
  that our passion is turned inward
  as deep within as a desert well.

Yet as guests at the waterfall of love
  we begin to awake
  to the passion of being hosts.
The water is not only for taking home
  from the well
  but for sharing on the spot.

In him whose thirst is still cracked lips
  pressed against a broken world,

TODAY'S SPIRITUALITY

we invite the Samaritans of our life
  to drink and splash and swim
in the waters of our shoreless bounty
  until the water trickles
  from the vulnerability of our concern
  merged with the blood
of our wounded love.

MANHATTAN MARY

MATT. 21:28-32   ". . . tax collectors and
                    prostitutes are entering the
                    kingdom of God before you."

Manhattan Mary.
  That's what they called her
  in the restaurant.
  Waitresses who winked knowingly,
  customers who smiled benignly.
It was a private joke,
  no snide snickers
  no caustic smirks.
A private joke whose public punchline
  was empathy.

You see, each day at noon
  Manhattan Mary
  (whose real name no one knew)
would enter the restaurant's main room
and go to her self-chosen booth.

Thomas R. Haney

There she'd order and sip,
   with delicate aplomb,
three manhattans while an hour
   drained away
and the pages of her book were turned slowly.

About one, Manhattan Mary
   would pay her bill quietly
   with a 15% tip and no fanfare.
Then with a slightly wobbly finesse
   she would steer across the room
   and leave.

Somehow,
   (no one seems to know exactly how,
   probably through pious osmosis
   some churchgoing people are gifted with)
a band of prominent members of the parish
   heard about her "scandalous" behavior.

Flustered with stony concern
   for the good name of the congregation
   (often the sacrament of sanctimony)
they first whispered worriedly
   among themselves
   then accosted their pastor.

"She can't come here any more,"
they purred at first with legal piety.
   "She doesn't belong!"
they shouted with argumentative rectitude.

TODAY'S SPIRITUALITY

"We don't want that type around,"
they confessed finally with honest hostility.

Their pastor went to his study
   that evening
   to pray over his scripture
   for Sunday's sermon.

His prayer didn't miss the irony of the text
   where Jesus stood on the borders of rage
   and spoke the sign language of contradiction,
"Tax collectors and prostitutes are entering
   the kingdom of God before you."

He heaved a sigh of heavy distraction
   and wondered where his mother would
   take communion next Sunday.

INVITATION

MATT. 22:1-14   "Go out into the byroads . . ."

The banquet hall was set
   the guests invited.
   In the byways of prejudice
a couple rejected their invitation
   refusing to budge
   from the brood of their excuses:

"The host is too long-winded
   and drones through the meal."

Thomas R. Haney

"The other guests are push-button robots
   uncritically attending
   any and all banquets."
"We don't like the setting
   there must be others
   more acceptable."
"The minstrels sing the same songs
   and often are as flat as the bread."

Still the Storyteller who
   ate and drank with sinners
   told stories of banquet halls filled
   with empty chairs to those
   who loved front seats
just as he had told tales of graves
   filled with dead men's bones
   to those who loved to splash
   around in whitewash
and had spun yarns about towns
   filled with dust
   shaken from the feet of mission
   to those who had turned up
   their noses at his feet
finally bathed in the tears of a prostitute.

Still the couple who had refused
   their invitation
   stood their ground where
living seeds had so often been trampled on.

Their friends who were attending the banquet
   paused over the excuses

TODAY'S SPIRITUALITY

as though their power of understanding
had been drained
at the touch of the couple's whining.

"Isn't part of the banquet," they asked,
"to extend peace to whatever
kinds of people are there
and to support the host in
his weaknesses?

Isn't the purpose of the banquet
forgiving seventy-times-seven times
and washing one another's feet?
Don't we come to give
as well as to receive?"

Still the couple scampered behind
the whited sepulchers of their excuses:
the atmosphere wasn't conducive,
they said,
to all these fine flights of appeals
to all these ideals of Samaritan love.

So the couple finally
made their way to another church
where they could hear Mass
offered by a priest
who fit the dictates of their eye-of-the-needle
preferences.

Thomas R. Haney

A SIGN OF CONTRADICTION

MATT. 25:1-13   "The reign of God can be
                   likened to ten bridesmaids . . ."

It was Ash Wednesday morning.
   He could hardly believe
   a whole year had gone by.
There would be no envelope this morning
   to carry ashes back to his mother
   to remind her that she was dust
   and unto dust she would return.
His mother had died this very morning.

Last Lent, he recalled, had been a good one.
   He had given up drinking
   for the whole six weeks,
   even on Sundays.
Then hardly had the first alleluias
   been sung when there he was,
   jubilantly drunk again.
His mother had cried and so had he.

Here, this morning, in his parish church,
   out of the corner of his awareness,
he thought he had heard the priest talking
   about the wise and foolish virgins
   (strange for such an occasion).

54

TODAY'S SPIRITUALITY

Suddenly, like a breeze off desert sands,
a realization swept over his brooding
(Was it the homily or his own notion?)

For the first time in his life
he realized that these virgins
were not merely characters
in a story.

No, they were the movements
of his soul,
the two sides of his character,
the wisdom and folly
of his choices.
He was the wise and foolish virgins!

There were times in his life
like during Lent, when
he was the wise virgins.
And those other times, most of the time,
when he was the foolish virgins.

His mother, confined to her bed
with time knocking, hammering
on the door of her soul,
would chide him gently,
"You should always be prepared
to meet your God."

With a smile, he would answer her
hiding behind a defensive quip,
"If I die during Lent, I'll be prepared."

Thomas R. Haney

Funny, he didn't, but she did —
   die during Lent, that is.
And no one was more prepared than she.
   She could have died on any day.

He walked forward and received
   the ashes on his forehead
   in the sign of contradiction.
He hoped he would not get depressed
   over his mother's death.
He always drank when he was depressed
   and that would be foolish,
   it being Lent and all.

HEART TO HEART

MARK 9:2-10   "He was well aware of what
                      was in man's heart."

Why is it, Lord, when I look
   into my heart
   I see myself straining gnats
   and swallowing camels,
   lengthening phylacteries
   and measuring an eye for an eye
while you see
   a widow's mite
   a little child
   a few fish
   a tiny seed
   and a hundredfold?

TODAY'S SPIRITUALITY

Why is it when I look into my heart
    I find whited sepulchers
    a brood of vipers
    and the glistening exterior of a washed cup
while you see
    the birds of the air
    the lilies of the field
    falling sparrows
    and wheat awaiting the harvester?

Why do I discover in my heart
    a king staring at a dancing girl
    who forfeits half a kingdom
    for a platter bloodied with a prophet's head
while you see
    fishermen who have forsaken all
    for a Vine whose branches
    stretch to the ends of the earth?

Why do I peer into my heart
    only to see myself
    standing in front of the temple
    pompously praying a recitation
    of self-serving virtues
while you see
    a woman bathing your feet
    in the precious ointment of humble repentance
    in the heartfelt tears of desolate sorrow?

Is it, Lord, that you can confront
    my schizophrenic heart
    and still call me friend

and utter your reassurance,
"Do not let your heart be troubled"
    so that on a Third Day somewhere
    I will be able to love
    with my whole heart?

Will I one day look into my heart
    and see myself standing
    around your altar-table
    where there will no longer be
    broken bread without broken hearts?

MAKING A DIFFERENCE

MARK 12:41-44   ". . . this poor widow contributed
                 more than all the others
                 who donated to the treasury."

How reckless!
    She could have kept
    one coin for herself.

How reckless!
    God could have continued
    to toss his prophets into
    the cauldron of the world's
    churning sinfulness
and kept his Son for himself.

TODAY'S SPIRITUALITY

How reckless!
    The Nazarene carpenter
    could have told his stories
    and kept his life for himself.

Maybe we measure too much.
    And maybe that's why
    we're not saints.

There's a certain recklessness
    to sanctity.

One that sacrifices both coins:
    the one of creativity
    the other of convenience.
Or on the opposite sides,
    imaginative planning for the future
    and hard work in the present.

And when we close the tight fist
    of fear around the coin of imagination
or the selfish fingers of annoyance
    around the coin of convenience
and when we bleat the self-pitying cry of
    "What can I do?"
maybe then, we know full well
    why we aren't saints.

Maybe we're willing to give
    but we hesitate because
    we think our coins won't make
    that much of a difference.

But in this story Jesus is chiding us
   into the belief that our contribution —
   no matter how small — to the
   overall impact for good in our world
does indeed make a difference.

Maybe, after all, sanctity is a recklessness
   that refuses to measure results.

THE TATTERED PRAYERBOOK

JOHN 17:1-11   "I entrusted to them the
                           message you entrusted
                           to me . . ."

He sat in what had been
   his mother's favorite chair.
Finally he opened her dog-eared
   prayerbook
   as he fingered her gold-rimmed
spectacles.

He read,
   trying to hear an echo of
   the message she had heard
   from that dutiful prayerbook,
but to no avail.

The message was there
   but his heart, hardened

60

TODAY'S SPIRITUALITY

by years of explosive ambition,
corroded by possessions, positions
   and power,
was not.

The story of Jesus reveals
   that the Word had
   entrusted the message
   to those who would receive it.

Beginning with the law and prophets
   not one iota would be changed
   until the message was fulfilled
   in those who had ears to hear,
eyes to see.

The prosperous son who
   had missed the funeral —
   the meeting in Switzerland
   had been of the utmost urgency —
had knocked on many doors in his lifetime:
   the doors of bankers
   the doors of industrialists
   the doors of scientists
   the doors of brokers.
"Knock and it shall be opened
   unto you," he had smiled wryly.

Now the words of his mother's prayerbook
   were like those
   written in the sand.

Thomas R. Haney

He closed the book,
   tossed it onto the hassock.
He placed the glasses on the table
   gently.
He looked at his watch.
   The plane from Global Oil
   was waiting for him.

''Another door,'' he sighed,
   glanced down at the book,
''Another time.''

THE HEALING WORD

LUKE 4:14-21   ''. . . and all were loud in
                           his praise.''

He was the teacher whose authority
   exploded out of the depths
   of God's tongue into a Word
   that would not return
until the deaf would hear and the mute would sing
   until even the stones would shout.
   And his audience was spellbound.

He was the healer whose power,
   like the creative finger of God
   touching clay into life and
   nudging life into community,
spoke words that dislodged spirits of evil

TODAY'S SPIRITUALITY

into prodigal shrieks.
And the onlookers were amazed.

The young woman said she felt lost,
   left out like a trickle of water
   dripping down the outside of an earthen jar
   whose contents had just mellowed
   into sweet, fragrant, abundant wine.

Her marriage, she now realized, had been
   sown in rocky ground,
had sprung up, flourished and died
   as suddenly as a boat
   sinks to the depths
   when there's no one around
   to walk the waves
   and calm the storm.
   And her friends were shocked.

She had sought counselling
   to exorcise the doubts
   eating away at her self-esteem
   like a psychic leprosy.
But the counselling she received
   only curved the thorns of doubt
   into a crown of piercing despair.
   And she felt more lost than ever.

Then one gracious day she re-read
   and pondered a story told by
   the teacher whose authority
   drove out serpents of evil.

Thomas R. Haney

Was she the lost coin in the story?
   Or the woman sweeping and searching?
   No matter.
   What was lost was retrieved.
And on the way she was finally healed.

Once more time split eternity
   and as if all yesterdays
   stood still in today
   the teacher's reputation spread again
through the young woman's unscrolled soul
   whereon the good news was as obvious
   as it had been so long ago
to the deaf who had heard it and the mute who had
   repeated it
   or to that poor possessed man
   whose shrieks of protest took wings
   on the notes of vaulting praise
   when he quaked under its expelling power
   that day in Capernaum's synagogue.
And those the young woman touched, believed.

COMING ALIVE

JOHN 11:1-45   "Lazarus, come forth."

We've been married 22 years.
   Things are not good between us.
   There're no fights or anything.
She's just indifferent.
   No matter what I do or say,

TODAY'S SPIRITUALITY

she's indifferent.
"It's not good between us."

We were discussing our favorite gospel stories.
He had chosen the one about Lazarus.
Now he was explaining.
"I keep thinking of myself standing there
at the tomb of our marriage,
calling to my wife.
It's like she's dead — to me, at least."

For him the story of Lazarus
had leaped from its tomb.
For us
if there's no crisis
no dilemma
no questions,
the story is familiarly bypassed
like a weed-covered grave
unmarked by our distracted busyness.

Yet the story of Lazarus doesn't
hang back there on the edge
of the First Century
("Isn't it wonderful what Jesus did!"
and then back to the daily grind).

Again and again the truth
collapses the barrier of time,
becomes the way that leads to life
and the truth is,
we are in Christ.

Thomas R. Haney

In Christ we have the power
   to sniff the air and smell death
   and break open tombs
   and call forth the dead:
   those perplexed and homeless
   those alone and hungry
   those unloved and confused.
We call forth those who languish
   in their underdeveloped potential,
   those who sleep away their goals,
   those who fear risk and
   hang like clinging vines to yesterdays.

When we stand before another's tomb
   and call,
   because we are in him
   and his power is in us,
the story of Jesus and Lazarus
   comes alive
for us and the unwrapping dead.

Others in Christ stand before my tomb
   and call to the dead in me:
      an imagination unused,
      a hope unloosed
      a love unlived
   they call to life again
      my talent for creative living
      my willingness to forgive
and finally,
      my acceptance of my dispensability.

TODAY'S SPIRITUALITY

The story of Lazarus
  becomes my story
  of Christ living in me.

LOVE

MATT. 22:34-40   "Teacher, which commandment
                    of the law is the greatest?"

He whose language boldly
  exploded with camels
  jumping through a needle's eye
  and mountains being
  hurled into the sea,
  when pressed,
fell back upon a quote:

"You shall love the Lord your God . . .
  and your neighbor as yourself."
Yet, as always, the quotation
  of revelation was made flesh
  in the story of him
who is the meaning incarnate of love:

Love
  pushes past whited sepulchers
  to quench its thirst
  at a sinner's well.

Thomas R. Haney

Love
    snaps the phylacteries
    of multiplied prayers
    to peek into a publican's plea,
"Lord, be merciful to me a sinner."

Love
    is the cock's crow
    tearing apart the night
    of fluent denials
echoing down through the tunnels
    of time,
a warning, a plea for tears.

Love
    is the crimson sin
    poured out in precious ointment
    on feet that marched to
    the rhythm of gnashing teeth.

Love
    is a cup passed,
    the phantom of blood
    spilling over Thabor's light
    in memory of one whose
foresight stretched back beyond
    Cain and chaos.

Love
    is a red night of explosive prayer
    reeling with ambitious hope
    in midnight spaces denied by day

TODAY'S SPIRITUALITY

where the words that one day would change
   meal into a sacrifice
   were first found and formed.

Love
   is the wine of suffering
   with the aftertaste of
   resurrection.

SEARCH FOR IDENTITY

LUKE 9:18-24   "Who do you say that I am?"
                       "You are the Messiah, the
                       Son of God."

An old man
   far spent in the rage for exactness,
   verbs dwindling to sighs,
   like a sheep with a whole grazing-day ahead.
No verb, graceful or dynamic, to ask,
   "Who am I?" or
   "Who do you say I am?"
Just retread adjectives,
   'old,' 'retired,' 'grandpop,' 'sick,' 'fishing.'

There was a wife a while back
   sometimes so real that he ached
   with the passion of recognition,
   sometimes so vague
   that it was like a fantasy
   moving in and out of dreams

Thomas R. Haney

as he dozed on the couch and coughed in the breeze.
It's funny how death can be so real
   and the dead such shadows.

It's better when you're younger to ask,
   "Who do you say I am?"
Instead of "What do you want me to do?"
   Life is so much clearer then
   especially when you know who you are
   before you know what you want to do.
It's better, too, before memory is a kaleidoscope
   piecing life into vagrant patterns
   that fall into the sky
   each day after day after grazing day.

Some say you're Jim.
Some say you're a widower.
Some say you're pop.
Some say you're an in-law.
Some say you're the old prof.
Some say you're a nuisance.
Some say you're wasting away.

   "But who do you say that I am?"

You're mine.
   You're precious.
      You're forever.

You're worth far more than
   the birds of the air,
   the lilies of the field,

TODAY'S SPIRITUALITY

the sparrows that fall,
the harvest that's ripe.
Why, you're worth
  nails and wood
  blood and water
  death and life
  bread and wine
  vine and branches.

But keep it to yourself
  because people can't see
  that far yet.
They like you up close where
  they can name you
  grip you
  control you
  and let you go.

But you're mine.
  You're precious.
  And you are forever.

Thomas R. Haney

WAYWARD AMBITION

LUKE 10:1-9
"... that we sit, one at your
right hand and the other at
your left."

Lord,
   James and John were just being
     practical.
   You kept talking about the reign
     that was to come
  the kingdom that was to be established
and they had an eye shrewder than most for
   the possibilities.
Judas could bounce the few coins
   hidden away in a purse of petty power.
James and John would gamble for a throne
   where they could make their importance felt.
Peter could ask in blustering innocence
   what was in it for those
   who had left everything.
James and John had already spotted
   the positions of power.

Lord,
   as always
  you reversed the whole process.
Real power did not reside
     in seats to the right and to the left

TODAY'S SPIRITUALITY

nor in lording it over others
nor in outward signs of prestige
nor in amassing the coins of the realm
nor in front places of honor.
James and John were not wrong
    in their judgment,
they were just displaced
and playing for high stakes
    in the wrong kingdom.

Lord,
    you reversed their expectations
    with the paradoxes of your kingdom
    where being first was being last
      being great was being servant
      being powerful was being meek
      being wise was being childlike
    where being found was being lost
      being saved was being sinner
      being honored was being crucified.

Lord,
    how often we are James and John
      pushing others aside
      for the inside track
    to a kingdom of our own making
    not of your coming.

How often we serve with the hope,
    in the guise of protesting humility,
    of being rewarded with honors
    which, it turns out very practically,

Thomas R. Haney

are no less petty than the coins of Judas.
How often our ambition for the coming
    of the kingdom
    is in fact our ambition for ascending
        to personal royalty.

Lord,
    help us to learn what it means
    to be meek and humble of heart
    that we may realize that
    kingship or queenship
    is bestowed through victimhood,
    that the power of your kingdom is exercised
        through personal sacrifice.

BELONGING

JOHN 10:11-18   "I have other sheep that do
                        not belong to this fold."

You know how it is.
    I was in church praying and
    someone's coughing, coughing, coughing.
Pretty soon I'm annoyed and
    pretty soon I'm not praying anymore.

Or the priest is preaching.
    The homily sounds prepared
    so I'm paying special attention and

TODAY'S SPIRITUALITY

a baby starts crying, crying, crying
   until my ears ring with agitation.
So I stop listening to the homily
   and the priest begins to stumble.

Jesus goes up to the Temple to pray and
   people come to him for instruction
   and church leaders come to question.
There's just no silence for him in the Temple.
There's just no listening for them in the Temple.

They come clapping the stone tablets of law
   in the ears of him who contests,
   "I teach only what I've heard
      from him who sent me
   because he and I are one."

They sit around drinking dark wine
   and talk of spilling blood
   because he who claims their God
      as his Father
   would lay no claims to messiahship
   wouldn't let them in on the know.

So he takes a walk on water
   where there are no Scribes or Pharisees,
      no soldiers or kings,
      no questions, no answers
      no wine and no blood
just water lapping around feet that
   leave no trace of the Way.

Thomas R. Haney

But he couldn't stay there long
   he had just gone out for a short breather
   so he goes back to the elbow-to-elbow
      noise in the Temple
   because after all he had said the other day
     "My sheep hear my voice
     and they follow me."
Anyway he had something to write on the sand.

Today I was in church again praying.
   I looked for the lady who coughed.
      She wasn't there.
Later in the petitions we were asked
   to pray for her.
      She had died during the week.

The young mother was there
   but her baby wasn't nor her husband.

It was quiet in church that day.
   I had no trouble trying to pray
   but somehow, I think, I had lost
      my way.

A SOMERSAULTING STORY

MATT. 13:1-23   "One day a farmer went out
                      sowing."

They gathered around,
    with God clenched in their fists
    like the soil from their farms,
    to listen to what a carpenter
    could tell them about farming
let alone about their God.

And so the carpenter told them that
    their God was a prodigal farmer
    with open hand
    casting seed to the four winds.

Well, they shuffled, all right so far.
    After all, their God, they knew, was
    a warrior, a pillar of light,
    a cloud, a judge, a lawgiver,
a tenfold plague on their enemies.
    They were comfortable
    and their God sounded familiar.

Then like a ringmaster
    who whistled all the cues
    he had his story do
    a somersault through

77

Thomas R. Haney

the hoop of their expectations
and land on its head
so that what was right-side-up
became upside-down.

The man of the first-as-last spoke.
  And you?
  Well, some of you look like soil
  but you are stony ground
  and others are thorny ground
  and others are as shallow
  as the shifting sands.
What takes root in you withers
  in the dust bowl of your souls.

He did it again! they protested.
  Turned an easy story
  into a hard saying.

Then the carpenter who knew about
  seeds that die to give life
  introduced another furrowed twist:
Some of you are good soil
  and you'll bear much grain.

Then a word of encouragement
  for those who had ears to hear:
Not all of you will bear
  the same amount of grain
  so don't get upset when you
  produce thirtyfold and
another bears sixtyfold or a hundredfold.

TODAY'S SPIRITUALITY

The story challenges us
   like a temple whip
   driving us out into the
   field of our lives to examine
what kind of soil we are.

The story transforms our discouragement
   into hope like water into wine
   as it allows thirtyfold
   to stand as ripe a harvest
   as a hundredfold.

AN UNANSWERED QUESTION

LUKE 3:10-15   "... wondering in their hearts
                 whether John might be the
                 Messiah."

It was raining
   the day he came to my door.
The clouds hung dark
   over my prayer for him,
   foreboding between us.
"I have a problem," he said.

He spoke the gray morning through.
   I listened and probed myself for
   what I might offer, what help,
what ray of hope in this overcast mood.

Thomas R. Haney

I'll be a presence, I thought
   but he wanted more,
   this pilgrim of the storm.
"What should I do?" he pleaded.

I stared at the ridges in his face
   and knew
   I was not the first he'd asked.

I bore my glance into the grooves
   beneath his brows
   and knew somehow
   he'd not listened before
   but he pressed me,
"Tell me, what should I do?"

The rain stopped
   the torrent of woe poured on
I felt drenched in helpless pity.
"What should I do?" he moaned.

Finally I suggested,
   "Why not go back
   to your daily seasons and contacts
   and try to be more honest
   with yourself?"

He stood and with a brusque nod
   moved toward the door.
"It looks like the rain's over," he said.

TODAY'S SPIRITUALITY

"I'm sorry," I replied —
  it was like a whine.
Then I mustered my faith
  and spoke out of the cloud
  of my own honesty,
  quietly, firmly, simply,
"I'm sorry, I am not the Messiah."

INNER-OUTER COLORS

MARK 1:40-45   "A leper approached Jesus . . ."

He had a very crooked nose
  and pointy ears
  and every recess
  he stood alone
except when the other children
  approached to taunt.

His eyes were clear and fixed
  deep and penetrating
  and that is why at home
  the tears overflowed so steadily
  from the crevices of his broken heart
because all the other children made such fun
  of his very crooked nose and pointy ears.

One day while he was standing alone in the recess
  yard
  an old gentleman came upon the scene.

Thomas R. Haney

"Why are you standing alone?" he asked
and the little boy with the very crooked nose and
   pointy ears
   looked astonished that this stranger
   had talked to him so gently.

"Well, you see sir," the little boy explained
   "I am different from other children
   and they don't like me
because, as you can see, I have a very crooked nose
   and pointy ears
   and my classmates love to make fun of me."

"Oh," the old gentleman said, "I see.
   Now let me show you something."
He removed his coat and showed the little boy
   his arm that was shorter almost than a toe
   with only two fingers like a tiny pair of pliers.

"When I was a little boy about your age,"
   the old man spoke ever so softly,
"no one would play with me either and
   people stared at me as though
   they had just paid their way into a sideshow."

"As I grew older," he went on, "I came to see
   that my other arm and hand
   were quite firm and strong
so I decided to learn how to draw and paint
   with colors that would match
the hues of nature's sunrises and sunsets."

TODAY'S SPIRITUALITY

"And did you learn?" the little boy asked
    with hope glistening in his eyes.
"If I may be immodest," the old man replied
    "I am a successful artist."

"You see, son, it is not how others see you
    that matters all that much.
It's really how you see yourself that counts the
    most,
        for people fail to look for inner beauty,
        for colors within that can make a rainbow
look like a dull gray streak in a forgotten,
    weeping sky."

Then as though a whisper had nestled in his ear
    the little boy with the very crooked nose and
    pointy ears
        began to sing.
His voice was like that of an angel winging
    heavenward
    and the old gentleman winked and walked on.
The little boy continued to sing through smiling lips
    as delicate and firm and full
    as an artist's fire-tipped brush.

Thomas R. Haney

THE GIFT OF HESITATION

LUKE 11:1-13   ". . . knock and it shall be
                                opened to you."

He paused at the door
   the familiar door of the church
   now so harsh with its blistered paint
   so unwelcoming, worn like the religion
   it hid behind its heavy lock, he mused.

What's the use? he muttered deep beneath
   his desperate need to ask once again
   in his measly-uttered prayer.
If he had kept a list of requests
   gone unanswered, it would stretch,
   he was certain, far beyond
   the longest cosmic joke in the universe.

Did God laugh? he wondered grimly.
   Yes, he decided, God had to laugh
   at the likes of his petty pleas.
His laughter had to roll with the impersonal echo
   of a storm-crazed ocean,
   he was certain.

His hand tightened on the knob of the door
   as his resolve not to enter
   the empty — or abandoned — church

84

TODAY'S SPIRITUALITY

hardened like cement, white as
his trembling knuckles fastened
to that door.

God! he whimpered into his own self-pity,
into the confines of his fragileness,
into the flood of his childish naivete,
into a past with no horizon.
God!

He turned from the door,
this man with a prayer
left unsaid, or so he thought.

As he turned he almost knocked over
a little old lady bundled
in her thin bones and threadbare shawl.
He apologized, bowed awkwardly and then
swung the heavy door open
for the lady, whose eyes said thank you.

Pray for me, he whispered long after
the rattle of her beads had softened
into the tomblike silence of the church.

Does God hear her prayers? he wondered.
Yes, yes, of course he does —
it was in her eyes,
this little old lady whom the world would regard
as a nobody
but whose prayer was heard.

Thomas R. Haney

Smiling he turned the knob
   only to discover the door was locked.
Gently he began to knock.

STRETCHED GRACE

MATT. 5:1-11   "Blessed are those
who mourn."

It had been months,
   months that moped along
   like inchworms with no particular
   goal to reach, just the slow, humping journey,
months since she had been to his grave.

At first she had gone each day,
   stood and cried until her
   eyes ached like an abscessed tooth
   and turned red like an October sunset.
Her husband warned her and scolded gently,
   "It won't change anything."
   "You're only doing damage to yourself."

It had been months too
   since she'd been to church.
When her husband asked if she wanted to go,
   she'd just retort with the anger
   of an accosting miracle-seeker,
"What kind of God would kill a little
   innocent child?"

86

TODAY'S SPIRITUALITY

It has been months and each day
   she'd recall the pastor's words —
   words that exploded like a cluster bomb
   in a heart too delicate to withstand a tremor —
"The Son of Man will come
   when you least expect him."

There were other days in those eternal months
   days more like moments,
   that flickered like fireflies,
   when she doubted her doubts.
Moments when she listened to other stories:
   the young widow whose husband
   had been struck down by lightning,
   the 80-year-old lady who
   still wept over a stillborn child,
   the tiny girl who clutched her doll
   and said her mother went home to God,
   the wife of a Vietnam MIA who lived
   on forced belief and shuddered at the future,
   the husband whose forbearance
   was tender and ever timely — her husband.

Gradually the stories stretched the moments
   into new, crisp months
   and transformed knuckle-angry
   resignation into open-handed initiative,
for in these stories the Author of life
   spoke to her about death
   until she discovered that
   every exit was an entrance
and that it was all right to grope.

Thomas R. Haney

One day with the help of the 80-year-old lady
   whose words were carved out of patient experience
   the bereaved mother wrote the following:
     "O God,
     Lord of the universe,
     I believe,
     despite all signs to the contrary,
     that you are drawing us all to yourself,
     to ultimate Simplicity that is total Unity
     and I am relieved."

The 80-year-old lady read the prayer,
   a smile curled pleasantly around her thought,
"The Son of Man does indeed come when you least
   expect him."

LOOK-ALIKES

MATT. 4:1-11   "... led into the desert
               ... to be tempted by the devil."

In the desert mirages are common
   like mirrors reflecting one's needs
   like the need for companionship.
Over there, for instance, a shadowy figure:
   man or mirage?
   friend or foe?
It's hard to tell in the desert.

TODAY'S SPIRITUALITY

In the desert there are such look-alikes:
    a temptation to self-serving ambition?
    or encouragement to noble feats?
    perverted zeal or idealistic motivations?
Such look-alikes
    like stones that look like loaves of bread
    like Spirit that looks like dove
    like wine that looks like water
    like blood that looks like wine.

It's hard to tell between look-alikes:
    Is it love or manipulation?
    hope or escapism?
    efficiency or noninvolvement?
professional judgments or squirming vengeances?
the spirit of poverty or disdainful righteousness?

In the desert the shadowy figure approaches,
    "If you are Son, is he then your Father?"
No, he is our Father."
    "If you are beloved, does that mean
    you cannot stub your toe
    on a temple pinnacle?"
    "No, it means I won't stumble
onto a cross
    rather I'll lay down my life
of my own accord."

In the desert the shadowy figure
    shifts like the sands,
    "Why not worship me?

Thomas R. Haney

Don't I look like 'our' Father?''
"No, you look like stones
trying to smell like bread
and stones and bread are not to be worshipped."

In today's desert look-alikes tempt us:
The desire for bread is made
to look like sin
when the only sin is unshared bread.

In today's desert
the shifting sand is expediency
and the shadowy figure still lies:
"Should you blame yourself
for bloated stomachs in far-off lands
just because you've earned your bread
by the sweat of your brow?

And so it is today
sin is made to look like
shrewd politics, astute business
until from El Salvador to South Africa
into Afghanistan
they are told not to worry about bread
because the dead don't eat bread
and they're riddled with bullets —
the modern version
of flesh-piercing nails.

REDIRECTED AMBITION

MARK 9:30-37   "... they had been arguing
                      with each other who was to
                      be the greatest."

Lord,
    you say to us in so many ways,
    "What does it profit a man if he
    gains the whole world and
    suffers the loss of his soul?"
Nothing marks the pathetic pettiness
    of my ambition more than the words,
    "the whole world."

I elbow my way through rank and file
    to get an edge and only intensify
    the edginess of my impatient ambition
    and recognize again and again
    in the dark of my frustration
that I never will come within a light year
    of gaining "the whole world."

Lord,
    in the shadow of your cross
    I may not wonder if I'm the greatest
    but I do fantasize about how great I am.

Thomas R. Haney

Ironically, Lord,
   in the wreckage of my petty ambition
   you issue your call
   to me to be great:
great in the service of others
great by being the servant of all
great by being first by being last.

Lord,
   you do not trample
the fallout of my exploded ambition to get ahead
   into the dust of false humility
rather you resurrect my ambition
   and transform it, recreated,
   into an ambitious meekness
   that recognizes the superiority of all others
   in and because of their need of service.

Lord,
   repeatedly you whisper
   "I have not come to be served
   but to serve,"
   and you continually challenge me
   to translate your words
   into your own common sense.

I do not ask any longer
   "How can I use others
   to further my own prestige?"
but I ask,
   "How can I place my talents
   at the service of others?"

TODAY'S SPIRITUALITY

Lord,
    grant us, the members of your Body,
    the insight, the conviction
    that the disputes and divisions
    that split us would be reduced
    if we would only serve
    rather than dominate,
    affirm rather than control,
fill the whole world with your loving concern
rather than try to gain the whole world
    for our own ambitious indifference.

A STORY OF JOURNEYS

LUKE 14:25-33   "Anyone who does not take up
                     his cross and follow me cannot
                     be my disciple."

She had stayed in France but
    made her home on the Euro-train.
Then played out by the work of travel
    she returned home to Washington, D.C.,
    where she was "practically given" a job
    in an embassy of a country she had not visited
    where she wrote speeches for
    various Egyptian dignitaries,
    helping the Arab mind to go
    from A to C through
    the B of English idiom.

Thomas R. Haney

Then, she said, one day she "hopped" into her car
   with her resume comfortably tucked
   into the passenger seat to travel into
   the world of televised newscasting.
Now she sat there engrossed in her interview
   pinpointing her incisive questions
   with the shy glamour of a debutante
and the gracious confidence of a knowledgeable
   journalist.
   She seemed settled now
   enjoying her new job
   as hurriedly as any settler
   of the Old West clearing the
   land of new adventure.

Even those who seem to have put
   down roots often breathe sighs
   of restlessness and look
   longingly through windows to
   horizons far beyond their destiny.

Perhaps these yearnings for
   endless journeyings are echoes
   of his invitation when he looked
   around the arid highways and byways
   of his native place and cried out,
"Come, follow me!"

But following him is a journey
   as perilous as trying
   to walk on water,

TODAY'S SPIRITUALITY

for no other reason than
it is a pilgrimage with a burden.

Not the burden of monogrammed suitcases
    filed with life's "necessities"
    nor trunks stashed with
    priceless family heirlooms.
No, the weight that presses our footsteps
    deep into the Golgotha road
    is that of crossbearing.

It is a journey that sets sights
    in such fierce determination that
    the pilgrim will turn her back
    on parents and loved ones
    but in the hope that they
    who view her back
    will follow her lead
    in footsteps already imprinted
    on the Way
    where those with burdens
    can come to him who refreshes.

THE HUMANNESS OF CHRIST

JOHN 14:8-11   "Lord, show us the Father . . ."

Finally it burst forth: The question.
    His memory swamped by divided waters,
    his imagination seared by the fires
        of the burning bush,

95

Thomas R. Haney

Philip blurted,
  "Show us the Father."

And he who bypassed the waters of Siloam
  that a paralytic might leap
    into the ecstasy of forgiveness,
  who squeezed clay mixed with spittle
  to fill blind eyes with rainbows,
  who broke a few loaves of perishable food
  into the promise of living bread
replied,
  "He who has seen me, has seen the Father."

Would they remember those words
  when they recalled how he had
  knelt at the feet of his creatures
  and divided water into a bath
    of loving service?
"He who has seen me, has seen the Father."

Would they remember those words
  when they touched the nail prints
  of the body that had hung
    mangled on the cross
twisted into an everlasting question mark?
  "He who has seen me, has seen the Father."

Would they remember those words
  when they asked in flame and wind
  what kind of a God he had really revealed?
A God who identifies with the least?
  The hungry, the imprisoned, the outcast?

TODAY'S SPIRITUALITY

A God who makes his home within us?
"He who has seen me, has seen the Father."

Perhaps the divine intimacy he revealed
is just too much for us.
Perhaps we're more comfortable
when we push the God he revealed
back onto his celestial throne,
a distant, disinterested, detached deity.
Perhaps we feel more pious when
we repaganize the Christian God.

But the story will not change
to suit our anxieties and fears
about disrespect,
to soothe our stretched pieties
or reward our rigid legalisms.

God became man
and wept bitter tears over Lazarus,
was amazed at the Centurion's faith,
fell asleep, exhausted, in a storm,
and called his creatures his friends.
The story tells us that the most damning disrespect
is to ignore the humanness which
revealed the intimacy of the divine.

"He who has seen me, has seen the Father."

Thomas R. Haney

THE GIFT OF THE OPPRESSED

JOHN 10:27-30   "My sheep hear my voice."

I stare at the picture taken
  only a few hundred miles
  but worlds away
from where I stand.
  The little child's vacant eyes
  dig like claws
into my helpless, volatile, snuffed heart.
  I am tortured.
How responsible am I for this child?
  And your words intrude
  like a nagging mea culpa,
"My sheep hear my voice.
  No one shall snatch them
  out of my hand."
And I am tortured into a scream of protest,
  What about this little lamb?

I gaze at the picture heavily and ask
  What can I do about
  this baby lying limp
  in his mother's scrawny arms,
  a careless bullet hole
  in his tiny breast?
And my question is another smooth stone
  slipped into the ever-growing

TODAY'S SPIRITUALITY

wall of my isolation
safely guarding me from responsibility
   from involvement, from caring finally.

The picture was taken, after all,
   worlds and worlds away.

You are risen and are Shepherd.
   Are you Shepherd "out there"?
A shadowy presence, an abstract Christ
   whose hands are a sheepfold
   emptied of snatched sheep?

Or is this what I need you to be
   so that I can curl up
   within my protests of helplessness
while I whine, estranged, in my freeze-dried piety?

You are risen and where are you now?
   Are you the bloated stomach
   of the child with a curable disease
   for whom there is no medicine
only a gun
   if he ever makes it to his future?

You are risen and are in me
   as I am in you.
Your work is now to pulsate through the veins
   of my efforts as surely as
   a branch, drawing its life and strength
   from the vine, produces fruit.

Thomas R. Haney

Whether I like it or not
it is now my hand, soft and manicured,
    that no one will snatch
    the sheep from.
That's what it has to mean when I exclaim
    "He is risen!"

And the picture I hold in my hand
    is no longer worlds away
but as close to me and as real as the words,
    "the Father and I are one."

PRETENSES TO PERFECTION

MATT. 5:17-20   ". . . unless your holiness
surpasses that of the scribes
and Pharisees . . ."

There are those who feel
    in the anxiety of their prayer
    in the torture of their efforts
that they are unworthy of God's love and mercy.

"I know what I will do," they say
    in tones reminiscent of the man
    who plotted bigger and better barns,
"I will preen my feathers until they're
    almost angelic in appearance.

I will polish my virtues until they dazzle
   like so many diadems in a halo.
I will make myself so lovable
   so desirable, so worthy, so attractive
   that the God of whimsical wrath
   and arbitrary judgment
will not be able to resist loving me.''

"I will make certain,'' they say, "that
   every cup is squeaky clean
   on the outside,
   that every tombstone glistens
   with the purity of whitewash,
   that no unclean food ever
   presses against my praying lips
that my face will frown and my hair be tossled
   with gruelling facts for all to see.
Then the God of iotas, jots and tittles
   will not be able to resist loving me.''

That's the spirituality of scribes and Pharisees
   said the man who was Word
   before any words were ever formed in prayer.
Let your holiness surpass that of
   the scribes and Pharisees
   said the man who was Holiness
   before grace ever stirred in any soul.

You know, said the man who was Love
   long before any creature ever rebelled,
I loved you always even when you were unlovable
   even while you still were sinners.

101

Thomas R. Haney

We emerge from the story of scribes and Pharisees,
   of a carpenter who was Creative Force
   long before an acorn stretched into an oak
   long before wood was nailed into a cross
and we know
   that our attention-getting devices
   are but the anxious gimmicks
   of a fearful faith, a terrified trust.

We know
   that Love, Mercy and Forgiveness
   are already present to our yearnings,
   are ours if only we surrender
our pretense to perfection.

FULFILLING THE LAW

MATT. 5:17-37   "Do not think I have come
                       to abolish the law. . . ."

He stood there,
   the chaff of Sabbath-picked grain
   at his feet like sawdust
   of an age long gone by.

He stood there
   responding to outstretched hands
   unwashed in purification rites
   reaching to be filled with the purity
   of a miraculous cure.

TODAY'S SPIRITUALITY

He stood there
   deep in Sabbath restrictions
   freely dispensing healing power
   to a man with a withered hand.

How then could this violator of the law
   claim,
"I have come to fulfill the law?"

His detractors
   were guides through
   a maze-like religion
   that demanded of followers
   picking their way
   through thousands of rules:

On the Sabbath could one carry food
   heavier than one dried fig
   or milk greater than one swallow?
On the Sabbath could a man lift a lamp
   from one place to another
   or a child from the floor
   to his knees?
On the Sabbath could someone write
   more than two letters
   of the alphabet?

We smile an all-knowing judgment
   at the pettiness of their legalisms
   until we remember that
   his fulfillment of the law
   is our challenge,

103

Thomas R. Haney

"Love one another as I have loved you."

Until we recognize how we fail
   to love one another with his love
   while we busy ourselves
   with rules and regulations
   that avoid the messiness
of dealing with those he's identified with
   and ignore his challenge
   to do to others as we would
   do to him.

Our question then becomes,
   How well do we
   fulfill his law?

RASH JUDGMENTS

LUKE 18:9-14   "Two men went up to the
                      Temple to pray . . ."

Lord,
   accused of eating and drinking with sinners,
   condemned as a glutton and drunkard,
at the touch of a tassle you healed the sick not the
   well.
   You told your story
   that the sinner might hear your call
and the self-righteous might never return home
   justified.

104

TODAY'S SPIRITUALITY

How quickly, humbly, readily, piously
  we identify with the fellow
  striking his breast in the rear of the Temple,
  with the elder son who worked hard
    and didn't squander
  with the Samaritan traveller who
    stopped and helped
  with the Magdelene who poured ointment
    and tears over your feet.

And perhaps in the very fantasy
  of identifying with them
we stand accused
  of our own self-righteousness.

We would never think of casting the first stone
  but we have no problem at all
  at being devoutly scandalized
  by those who do not measure up
  to our version of external conformity
  to our stereotype of propriety.

Like a chameleon
  self-righteousness can take on
  a rainbow of colorful virtues
and sanctimony can so smoothly purr
  such pious protestations:

"I'm not condemning him
  but did you see the way he behaved?"
"It's not for me to judge
  but I can't believe she said that!"

Thomas R. Haney

"Well, I must admit I expected
    more from him."
"I've never been so shocked . . ."
"I'm simply at a loss for words . . ."
"Of course, you heard about . . ."
"Oh, I can't believe that about him
    but it must be true."

We'd never dream of thanking God
    that we're not like the rest.
It's much more reassuring, comfortable,
    pious to stand in the back
    and strike our breasts
while clutching a stone in the other hand.

The tragedy of the man up in the front line of
    the Temple was
    that he went home utterly convinced
    that he was the one who was justified.

Our tragedy is
    that we'll never be convinced
    that our unadmitted self-righteousness
destroys the unity of the Body
    dissipates the Spirit of love
and negates our imitation of God
    who loved us first
    even while we were sinners.

RIGHTEOUS SIN

JOHN 20:19-23   "Whose sins you shall forgive
they are forgiven them."

The 6:30 a.m. Mass was his
  as surely as the morning sky
  belonged to the rising sun.
He attended with the fierce dedication
  of a meticulous bookkeeper
  engraving scrupulous pluses and minuses
  in strict, eye-for-an-eye columns.

Every Sunday morning at 6:30 Mass
  he passed the basket with
  unsmiling intensity even among those
  who stood across the street
  fulfilling their obligation long-distance
but close enough to avoid the ire of Hell.

  Sometimes the breath must blow like
  a driving wind just to get inside.

As faithful as he was to the 6:30 Mass
  so he was just as steadfast
  to the judgment he had passed on his daughter
  for whom he always had a stone in hand
for the disgrace she had spread like a dark stain
  over his family's embarrassed reputation.

107

Thomas R. Haney

He remembered it like yesterday although it was
    now
    ten years or more ago
    and he remembered each and every day.
    It was the bile that soured his every prayer.
    She had stood there and announced
    her marriage to that divorced man
    and he knew it had been outside the Church.
"Out!" he had screamed his excommunication
and turned his back on the closing door.

    Sinners need forgiveness
    if sin is to be forgiven.

His heart slammed him to the ground
    one ordinary grass-cutting afternoon
    when the face of the earth was being renewed.
The eerie siren proclaimed to the medical community
    deep in the emergency tunnel that
    all their marvels of survival
    were in the end tentative forestallings.

He lay still as death while the beep of the monitor
    insisted the signs of life were vital.

Crouched by his bed was his daughter of years ago,
    her tears dropping on the hand
that had crashed like a gavel of final judgment
    and her sobs pleaded, "Forgive." "Accept."
Suddenly she felt that hand grasp hers as though
    gripping a staff for the last leg of a journey,
    heard the final rush of breath, saw the smile

and knew the fire of love rekindled in the cold of
limp death.

The beginning was all over
and what was all over was just beginning.

FAITH

JOHN 6:60-69   "From this time on, many of
                      his disciples broke away and
                      would not remain in his
                      company any longer."

They caught the words
   of high romance
   and buried them deep
   in the thorny ground of their hearts,
these Chosen People.

He promised them the intimacy
   of a bread alive with divinizing yeast:
"I myself am the living bread"
   and like builders of a verbal labyrinth
   they quarreled over the "how"
when the real question flashed
   in the infinity of the "why."

They wanted a God whose fiery chariot
   would crush the oppressor
   under the wheels of righteousness.

109

Thomas R. Haney

A God who'd guard each letter of the law
   like the prissy museum curator
and they were told that God is as soft
   as dough, as loose as wine.

They prodded him, "Dance on the pinhead
   of a miracle for us:
   spit on clay that the blind might see
   break bread and feed thousands
   kneel in prayer that the lame might leap
   walk on water and turn it into wine
but don't talk to us about
   flesh that smells like bread."

Finally, they walked away
   these Chosen People.

"I would not have walked away.
I would have believed
   had I been there," you claim.
But you had the advantage
   of hearing about the supper
   before you heard about the promise.
What's done is less a challenge
   than what's promised.
Besides, which is less grateful,
   to walk away in doubt
   or to walk forward in indifference?
   an empty ritual
   or honest questions?

TODAY'S SPIRITUALITY

The Pharisee went home from the temple
   unjustified not because his prayer
   wasn't liturgically exact and precise,
   but because his prayer addressed
   the absence of God and
   the presence of his own ego.
God had merely been a magnifying glass
   to enlarge his righteousness.
The Pharisee had tried to control the
   Uncontrollable.

There's more to accepting the living bread
   than just being there.
Faith is more than not walking away.

CHARCOAL BURN-OUT

MATT. 6:24-34   "Today has troubles enough
                   of its own."

In a clinically abstract office,
   a square cubicle for edgeless minds,
   lifeless but for vibrations
   of staccato probings
   and psychoanalytical syllables,
she finally confessed
   her burn-out.

Finally she admitted to the analyst
   as though talking out loud
to herself.

Thomas R. Haney

"My God, my schedule was suicidal."
Her tears hung like iced raindrops.

She hesitated as though afraid
 to turn back the pages of a diary.
"My scattered efforts blurred into
 a mishmash
 of today's struggles and tomorrow's anxieties.
Worry shook my sleepless bed at night
 like a diabolical obsession
 and my prayer was like a burned-out candle."

"Being a religious person," responded the analyst
 whose business was sanity,
"You're familiar with the gospel lesson
 about not being anxious?"

"You mean," said the lady of the burn-out,
" 'wing it' like the birds of the air,
 blossom where you're planted
 like the lilies of the field?"

"The story helped for a while," she admitted
 until I began reading it
 through the Third World eyes
 of survivors who can't fret
about tomorrow
 because today may be all they have.
"And there I was," her voice drifted off
 into the vacuum where her
 global burdens were once piled.

TODAY'S SPIRITUALITY

"There's a line in that story,"
  the analyst prodded,
'Sufficient for the day is the trouble therein,'
  Can you live with that?

One day's problems at a time?"
  His words fell like bait
  into the tortured emptiness
  where once had been flowing water
  for all who were parched.

"Is there an image you'd use
  to describe your burn-out?"
  asked the analyst
  whose business was sanity.

"Yes," said the lady of the burn-out.
  "I feel charcoal dry."
A smile shrugged across her tense lips
  for the first time that afternoon.
"But, then, charcoal burns too,
  doesn't it?"

Thomas R. Haney

THE SECRET

MARK 1:21-28   ". . . he entered the synagogue
       and taught."

"He's got a devil in 'im"
 they all shouted
like thunder rolling off mountain peaks.

"He's quite mad, you know," the village doctor
 observed.
 "And he could be dangerous,"
 a housewife whispered
 as she washed suds from her hands.

But the one they spoke of just sat there
 under the oak tree
 smiling, smiling, smiling
 as if he had a secret
 he could never tell.

Now it happened one day that a healer
 from the medicine show
 came to town with bottles
 jingling their nectar of health.

"Come and see him," the townsfolk persuaded.
 "Come and see how mad he is!"

114

TODAY'S SPIRITUALITY

The healer approached and found him
   sitting there under the oak
   smiling, smiling, smiling
   as if he had a secret
   he could never tell.

"Yes," the healer agreed, "there can be no doubt.
   He is indeed quite mad."
And the healer walked away shrugging his shoulders
   leaving the villagers to their own dismay.

That night when all were in bed
   a wailing sound arose,
   a child's cry of anguish,
   yet no one heard but the one
   who sat beneath the oak tree
   smiling, smiling, smiling.

As the cry grew louder, he who was thought to be
   mad
   rose and lumbered toward the child
   who was caught in a trap set for wolves.

With strength beyond human belief
   he tore the trap apart,
   lifted the child to his shoulders
and whispered words to soothe the wound.

Then he took the child to the doctor's home
   and placed him gently
   on the worn stoop
   and knocked loudly on the door.

115

Thomas R. Haney

The next day the doctor told the story about
  how he who was thought to be mad
  had brought the wounded child to his home
and all the villagers accused the one who sat
  smiling, smiling, smiling
  of mutilating the helpless child
  who had wailed in the night.

With heavy clubs they beat the one thought mad
  'til he smiled no more
  and then went home
  certain that an exorcism had been done.

And when the little child whom he had saved
  grew tall and strong,
  he sat beneath the oak tree
  smiling, smiling, smiling
  as if he had a secret
  he could never tell.

COUNTERCULTURAL SPIRITUALITY

MATT. 5:1-11
    "Blessed are the poor for theirs is the Kingdom of heaven."

Some smiled upward toward the sky
  through rags and sores,
  the bones of their emaciated neglect
  cracked with joy at his words.

116

Others — the ones in the know — frowned
   through their riches,
   they shuffled their feet
   and milled around
   backing against the tablets of the Law,
   pulling proverbs from the deep pockets
   of their phylacteries to prove
   that the truly chosen people were rich
   in land and sons —
   signs of Yahweh's favor.

"Who can bear the burden of this hard teaching?"
   they cried out angrily.
Only the unfavored poor would enshrine poverty.
Only the disenfranchised would claim the kingdom
   with such carelessness.

Anyway, what does he know about kingdoms?
He doesn't even have a place to lay his head!
   They pick up stones.
   "Let's kill him," they whisper,
   but not today — it's the Sabbath.

It's not easy to live a spirituality
   of cultural resistance.
To stand before the tribunal of Officialdom
   and try to answer the question,
   "What is truth?"
To be scourged with the thongs of scorn
   crowned with the thorns of contempt.

We know how we feel

Thomas R. Haney

when our lifestyle protests
a greed that makes the world
safe for investment.
We know how the gospel is quoted against us:
"The poor you shall always
have with you"
and ridicule chokes our sincerity
and deals a damaging question
to our patriotism.

But he persists:
the kingdom belongs to the poor
who do not envy the rich
to the ones who give away coat and overcoat
who put a beaten traveller up
at an inn and pay with excommunicated coin,
who offer a few loaves
for a blessed multiplication,
who unostentatiously drop a mite
in the collection basket.
These will breeze through the needle's eye
into the kingdom.

And then he turns to us
with a glance that evokes tears
and asks,
"Will you also go away?"
which translates,
Will you allow your religion to degenerate
into a decent formula
wherewith to embellish
a comfortable life?

TODAY'S SPIRITUALITY

CELEBRATING THE TRINITY

MATT. 28:16-20

". . . baptizing them in the
name of the Father and of
the Son and of the Holy
Spirit . . ."

Lord, God, Creator,
    Master of immensity,
    Artist of intricacies,
    out of nothing, everything.
    Thousands of galaxies
    millions of rose petals.
I look at your midnight sky
    and explode with the feeling
    of a fleeting fleck
    within your vast expanse.
I gaze intently at the labyrinth
    of a rose's interior
    and am absorbed into
    your creative wonder.

Yes, Lord, God in Trinity,
    I ask why for so long
    I allowed you to lie sideways
    in the captured concepts of
    Persons and Nature,
unexperienced like musical notes caught silent
    on the bars of an unplayed score.

Thomas R. Haney

Lord,
    why for so long did I carry you
    in the fragile memories
    of heavy studies of bookish learning
    while you were revealing your intimacy
    in stories
    of lost coins and wandering sheep,
    of robbed pilgrims and hapless sons,
    of eleventh-hour coin and hidden weeds,
    stories which break open the mystery
to reveal that your home is human life.

Your Son, Lord,
    announced his purpose,
    "I have come that they may
    have life and life to the full."
Your Spirit, Lord,
    blessed us with the insight
    that where your life is
    there you are,
Father, Son and Spirit,
    Trinity making your home
    within us.

Lord,
    grant me
    in the aimless void
    of my nothingness
    which opens into
    the deepest reaches
    of my innermost self
    the mystic wordlessness,

TODAY'S SPIRITUALITY

the breathless silence
where Mystery dwells deep down
where I can touch the totality of reality
where I can experience you
dwelling within me
three Persons in one Nature,
Father, Son and Spirit,
indwelling Trinity.

INCALCULABLE FORGIVENESS

MATT. 18:21-35   ". . . not seven times; I say,
                        seventy times seven times."

In the grudging precision
   of mathematical equations
   the search for perfection
   falters
   and finally fades
   in the white epiphany
of a covenant cup:

"How often do I forgive?
   Seven times?"

"No, love will not tolerate
   the limits of a ledger's edge
   and no human accounting
   will contain these numbers,
seventy times seven times."

Thomas R. Haney

The words smart like a bee sting
  on the hand
  of one who would calculate
  spiritual achievements
  like the multiplication table,
seventy times seven times.

The ideal darkens the confident brow
  of one who would measure
  mystic experience
  as some form of calculus
  and equate
human lapses with just retributions.

Seven times is much simpler
  to count and record
  on the chalkboard
  of mortal frailty
and brings blessed relief from
  the terror of endless forgiving.

What the fisherman who had spent
  his life counting his catch
  failed to factor into
  the equation of reconciliation
  was that the one whose
  numbers were infinite
  came as Word not numeral
and the Word is Forgiveness.

THE GIFT OF LOSS

LUKE 2:41-52   "The child Jesus remained
                     behind. . . . Not finding him
                     they returned to Jerusalem. . . ."

Ivan Illych was his name
    and Leo Tolstoy penned
    him into the parables of our times
    to disturb our neatly typed lives
and force us to look askance at our assumptions.

For Ivan Illych, so Tolstoy's story goes,
    had always done the correct thing:
    he had taken the right job
    he had married the right woman
    he had the requisite number of children
    he had all the correct connections
and did everything that was expected of him
    all his life long.

Now Ivan Illych is on his deathbed
    and fears his life was a waste
    for, you see, he had been so busy
    doing all the correct things
that his life had slipped by
    without a flicker of passion.

Thomas R. Haney

The parable ends, as all parables must,
   upsetting our comfortable assumptions
   about living a correct life
   in a passionless sort of way
   and asking in an unwritten question,
"Why not correct the correctness of your life?"

Lord,
   let us enter your story
   that we might reshape our story.

Now those who taught the correctness
   of the Law within the Temple school
   sat instructing a young boy
   whose passion for the truth
   allowed for a breach of the correctness
   of returning home at festival's end
   and whose passion for his Father's house
prompted visions of a Temple destroyed
   and rebuilt within three days.

The days would come as sure as lightning across the
   sky
   when those whose tongues were like
   unrolled scrolls of the Law
   would accuse him of violating
   the correctness of not eating with sinners
   and damn him a drunkard and a glutton
because his passion for the lost knew no propriety.

Undaunted,
   he would go on telling stories

TODAY'S SPIRITUALITY

of loss that people might know
that life is a search joined
by God the Good Housekeeper
who sweeps and cleans and seeks
with the frantic passion of a woman
who will ignore the correctness even of the Sabbath
    law
until she finds the coin that was lost.

And we repeat and retell his stories
    until they stir our passion
    for cleaning the inside
    as well as the outside of the cup,
    until the correctness of our lives
    reflects the truth of our stories,
    until we lose ourselves
    in the mystery of the living Temple.

LOCKSTEP PROPHETESS

LUKE 21:5-19   ". . . not one stone will be
                                left on another. . . ."

She pulled me into
    the word processor of
    her biblical memory
where passages from The Book
    clicked with
    computerized precision,
    with the printout fervor
of pamphleteering zeal.

Thomas R. Haney

"You know what
the Bible says,"
her words an archangelic announcement,
    a springboard for her plunge
    into Revelation
that she might break the scriptural surface
    with a quotation
    clenched in her teeth,
"'. . . the day will come when not one stone
    will be left on another. . . .'"

She stood there thrilled in her prophetic rage,
    her only context her own security,
her finger jabbing like a demon-expelling wand.
    "You with your latter-day temples
    'adorned with precious stones
    and votive offerings'
    with your idolatrous statues and
    your superstitious sacrament,"
her voice thundered like an echo
    from Jacob's well,
    "You will have to answer one day
    the Bible's question,
"When the Son of Man comes, will he find
    faith on earth?"

"Or," her eyes flashed wide
    with apocalyptic menace,
"will he find your churches empty
    monuments to the failures
    of your man-made rituals,
    your lips screaming his name

but your hearts far from him?
This is all you need!"
   and she thrust The Book
   into the air as though some
invisible hand might reach down
   and snatch it in a wild
   divine act of ownership.

In the ensuing messy silence
   following her departure
I made my weary, uneasy way to the church.
   The thought that came to mind
   was not strictly from the Bible
   (and perhaps that's why
   she was unaware of it):
"We need sacred places and holy times
   so that we will recognize
   all places as sacred
   all times as holy."

NO AUTOMATIC ENTRANCE

LUKE 13:22-30   "Try to come in through the
                       narrow door."

No wonder they tried to push
   him off the edge of a cliff.
They were the first to refuse to worship
   idols that had eyes
   but no all-seeing providence,

idols that had ears
stone deaf to praise or petitions.

They were the first to observe the law
even to the distortions of its letter,
even if it meant measuring others' sins
while calculating their own merits
and casting stones of condemnation
with an eye-for-an-eye accuracy.

And now he tells them with the simplicity
of one who writes his legacy
in the shifting sands
that the first shall be last
that the self-sufficient would beg
in the bowels of eternity
for a fingertip of water
and watch their overstuffed barns
fade away in the failing sight of death.

If those who dared the tightrope
of legalistic observance
could fall from the heights
of sanctimony,
then who could enter the narrow door?

Will it be those who stand
in the front of the Temple
parading their virtues
while nursing judgments
against those who stand
in the rear and pray?

TODAY'S SPIRITUALITY

If indeed the first shall be last
  will not the Lord of paradox
  move those who prowl
  the vestibules of temples
  up into the sanctuaries?

Will they enter the narrow door
  who cry out, "Lord, Lord!"
  and bypass the traveler in the ditch,
  who pray on street corners
  while they bind burdens
for the backs of those deemed less worthy?

These are hard sayings, they clamored.
  What kind of a God prefers
  mercy that cannot be measured
  to butchered bullocks and burnt lambs
  in liturgies so easily numbered
  for his glory?

He bowed his shoulders like a farmer
  who grips his plough
  with no backward glances
  and pushed his way toward Jerusalem
  with Calvary in his blood
  and the rolled-back stone in his heart.
The narrow door would have to be opened.

Thomas R. Haney

THE GIFT OF FREEDOM

JOHN 3:1-21   "A certain Pharisee named
                          Nicodemus . . . came to him
                          at night."

"Do you want a token for
    a car wash or a raincheck?"
he would ask if you filled
your tank with gas.

She walked toward her car
    examining the raincheck
intently
    smiling the quizzical smile
    we all do
    whenever we get something free.

Water and Spirit are free
    said the Man from the Jordan.
But Nicodemus frowned a shocked question:
    "Is a free rebirth like
    swallowing a camel?
    Can a hump pass through the throat
    any easier than a man can
reenter his mother's womb?"

"One thing is necessary,"
    lectured the promo expert,

130

TODAY'S SPIRITUALITY

"if you want to create a consumer need:
   the illusion of scarcity."

"I am with you always
   until the end of time,"
   said the Man of all-night vigils.
But the night of Nicodemus'
   prayerful search
   revealed no scarcity
when a God of such availability
   was so easily accessible.

In the darkness
   we join with Nicodemus
   and ask
   "Where's the gimmick?"

Free gifts floating down
   like the birds of the air
   are hard to see at night.
Free gifts, as unearned as the beauty
   of the lilies of the field,
   look a lot like weeds
creeping up and choking wheat
   at night.

So we stand in the night
   of our cock's crowing,
   knee-deep in Nicodemus' doubt,
and question the unconditional love
   even of the Man
who freely laid down his life and asked,

Thomas R. Haney

"Do you believe this?"

Yet if the wild berry and the fresh air
   elude the dark drawer
   of the cash register,
why do we take a raincheck
   from the Man of the Third Day
   who deluges us with
   purifying gifts?
Is it that we have yet to accept
   the gift of our freedom?

THE PRODIGAL

LUKE 15:11-24   "A certain man had two sons."

"You'll go to church
   as long as you're under this roof!"
His voice snapped like a temple whip
   and his eyes glared like Sinai at sunset.

And so his son rolled out from under the roof
   and settled like a coin lost in a corner
   of a sacristy.

And his father knelt in anger
   and prayed a hard prayer
   as proper as any rubric demands
of anyone whose righteous pain
   is soothed by knowing
   he was right

TODAY'S SPIRITUALITY

in severing the bond of human love
   and calling it the divine will.

He read his Bible and knew
   the parable of fatherly forgiveness
   was reserved
   for repentant sons.

Meanwhile his older son
   "a good boy"
went to church and prayed and sang
   while at night
   he trafficked in drugs
and gambled his father's check
   in furtive moans
   and 'next-time' pain.

His father read his Bible and knew
   no fatted forgiveness
   was needed for a son
   who always went to church.

How strangely sad the sight
   of those who read the Bible
   like a dishwasher scrutinizing
   the outside of a cup.

How strangely judicious are they who rework
   the teachings of the gospel
   like a lawyer getting his guilty client off
   on a technicality of legalistic subtlety.

Thomas R. Haney

And, as lost as a wayward sheep,
  is the story
  of the joyful tears of a dusty boy
  and a father who ran into the arms of sin
because the ways of God
  are the topsy-turvey opposite
  of the ways of human righteousness,
because divine forgiveness begins
  before human sin occurs
since the road of sin is the same
  as the road of repentance.

THE DOORBELL

MARK 12:28-34   "You shall love your neighbor
    as yourself."

Lord,
  I am now the one
  asking the question,
"Which is the greatest of all the
    commandments?"

And suddenly I'm on the dusty road
to Jericho.
I have three passes.

First I hurry by the wounded traveler,
  caught up in the busyness
  of my legalistic duty.

134

TODAY'S SPIRITUALITY

You give me another chance.
  This time I walk by
  lost in the pursuit of my goal
  preoccupied with my lot in life.
Finally on my third pass
  I stop and this time
  I take a long, soft look.

There in the ditch, a human being
  with a unique personal history,
  with a divine plan imprinted
  in his individual talents
  who like most human beings
  is taken for granted, ignored, disposable
and carelessly wasted.

"For the love of God, love me," he cries.
  He cries out to me.

The scene changes.
  I am now in the comfort of my study
  in an early morning hour
  before the world awakens
  to the pursuit of daylight goals.
  I hear a moan outside my window.
  "Help me,"
  and the doorbell rings and rings.
I know I can sit and pray
  that whoever it is will go away
  so that I won't have to stoop down
  and scoop up a tragedy into my concern.

Thomas R. Haney

It may be a drunk
   or someone who's been mugged
   or a junkie high on danger
   or someone who just won't make sense
   or a threat of some grotesque sort.

The bell rings and rings
   like the knocking of the neighbor
   who wants to borrow bread
   at some ungodly hour
until bread is shared in a Godly moment.

Finally I go down to the door
   and the 4 a.m. visitor
   asks directions to another part of town.
He thanks me and apologizes for the bother
   and I climb the stairs
   wondering which of us is lost.

Lord,
   I know the answer.
   It's been there all the while:
"For the love of God, love me
   in the refuse of my disposed-of-images.
Love me in the human disruptions of your busy life.

   Love me
   in the ditches of your world
   at the doorbells of wayward pilgrimages."

TODAY'S SPIRITUALITY

THE MIRACULOUS VEIL

JOHN 6:32-40   "I myself am the bread of life."

The priest said he didn't
  have an opinion, really.
He said we should be careful
  not to run after extraordinary
  signs and wonders like this veil
  with the picture of Christ's face on it.

I thought of going over for a look-see.
  A veil whose folds hang like
  creases of Christ's face.
A divine finger-painting rising
  out of a tabernacle shroud.
But instead I kicked a pebble
  and thought of Abraham
  and his descendants
  from the stones laying around our feet.
Signs and wonders can be deceiving.

Signs have been posted, I figured, all
  along the jagged syllables
  of revelation.

But like Burma Shave signs down
  the highway, the God-signs pass by
  before we barely begin to notice.

Thomas R. Haney

I don't know where I was but
  the next thing I knew we were
  standing up for the Our Father.

I guess that's why people
  stand in rosary bead lines
  waiting like latter-day Veronicas
  to gasp at the veiled image
  of a God who finally threw himself
  off the temple pinnacle.

Somehow a God as unpretentious
  as the bread we eat
  or as available as communion lines
  isn't any more marvelous than
  a carpenter who refuses to bake
  bread out of the dough of desert stones.

Somehow a God who stoops to wash
  the mission feet that had tramped
  around in sin and sickness
  makes us walk away looking for
a God who hangs like a puppet
  on the strings of our expectations.
"You're going to be the God we want you
  to be, not the God you want to be."

And so we shove and push through
  the decades of people
  to get a glimpse of a God
whose portrait hangs over a reality

TODAY'S SPIRITUALITY

that looks only like bread —
even if the Sign said it's living bread.

THE FLOURISHING SEED

JOHN 12:20-33   "The hour has come . . . unless
                       the grain of wheat falls to
                       the earth and dies it remains
                       just a grain of wheat."

The hour of Cana briefly resisted
  in playful charm with her
  whose life broke into weddings
like the angel who had invaded her dreams
  so long ago with words
  of a Spirit that enlightens
  as it overshadows
and a God whose Word is the seed of the
  Most High —
  that hour has now come.

It was not the hour of loaves and fishes
  spread like picnic
  and feasted upon like banquet
  nor the hour when waves bowed
  to the soft tread of reassuring footsteps.

It was not the hour of carpeting palms
  and stones ready to join in a chorus
  of revealing hosannas.

Thomas R. Haney

It was not the hour of mountainpeak garments
   shining like sun-filtered snow
   and a headline vision embargoed
   'til Life burst through the finished touches
   of nails and lance
   and prowled the garden of risen hope.

It was the hour of the solitary seed reborn like
   summer
   out of the death of winter
   and the fertile joy of spring
emblazoning the horizon with a hundredfold harvest
   and it is your hour
   as well as his.

The hour has come for you
   and it is not unlike his.
Often the hour that has come is
   like standing alone on a precipice.
   You are there and no one else
   will approach and stand with you.
You are alone
and yet you celebrate.

Or the hour that has come is like reading ahead
   when everyone else is dilly-dallying
   on the first page of study
   or satisfied with an unopened book.
You are alone
and yet you celebrate.

TODAY'S SPIRITUALITY

Or the hour has come and you are willing to risk,
    to follow the swish of the Spirit
    who blows where he will
    even at times like a raging storm
    when others stand secure quoting rules
    judging you by standards
    as arbitrary as hunches.
You are alone
and yet you celebrate.

You are alone
but warm in the fertile soil
    of Providence
    like a seed
    one day to be
    a hundredfold
    and you celebrate
even though the harvest may be far off.

LIFE ON THE ALTAR

JOHN 10:11-18   "... the good shepherd lays
                      down his life for the sheep."

He saved my life
    in that jungle now entwined
    in my gnarled memory of wars
    and rumors of war,
in that jungle where Agent Orange
    was the sniper, the unknown enemy.

141

Thomas R. Haney

He was our Sergeant
  whose smile was as crooked
  as the trails where body counts
  were the only signposts to
  uncertain victory,
  whose heart carried more battles
  than heartbeats,
whose love for us was a rugged curse.

What happened was as swift and baffling
  as a surgeon's scalpel
plunging into a hemorrhaging organ.
  I felt the weight of his body
  crush me to the mud
  with the force of an overturned jeep
  and heard what sounded like
  a muffled sneeze
and felt the unmistakable quake
  of an exploding bomb.

Later as I sat in the daze of bewilderment
  staring at the scarlet gash
  where once the crooked smile had been
  I remembered hearing words
  on the hushed lips of our padre,
"Greater love no one has than to lay down
  his life for his friends."

I thought of him tonight
  as I paced back and forth
  in lost sleep
  hugging my fevered child

142

TODAY'S SPIRITUALITY

close to my hot breath
clutching him like a
new-found treasure
trembling with the premonition
that precious jewels are made
    not of stone but of flesh
    and I prayed
for the first time, I think, since coming home.

Now, as I reflect, I realize
    that life has meaning
    only when it is placed
    on the altar of sacrifice,
and what takes life away is the self-pity
    that poisons with the finality
    of those mists of Agent Orange
which no hero's body could ever cover.

LETTING GO

LUKE 4:14-21   ". . . to proclaim liberty to
                                captives."

He stood there,
    the smell of wood still clinging
    to his skin like incarnation
    to his divinity,
the scroll in his rough-hewn hands
    unfurled like a flag
of one testament's surrender to another.

143

Thomas R. Haney

They sat in synagogue silence,
   their tradition sealed away
   in memory
   as though it were in a bank vault
   for which there was no key.

The carpenter sat and taught,
   "The Lord's year of favor
   is upon you now,
   all captives are to be set free,"
   and his words fell trembling
into the fertile soil of amazement
   until they were finally choked
   by the anger of vested interest,
   "We know who you are.
   By what authority do you teach us?"

And the year of favor seemed most
   unfavorable to the Word
   who had just announced it.

Now we hear his words
   and we twitch uncomfortably
   at the thought of letting captives go.
   All the long hours spent
   in gaining control over those
   whose capture bolstered our egos
   would somehow dwindle to a single tick
in a year-long stretch of the Lord's favor.

The mother whose moan of feigned pain
   kept her daughter

144

TODAY'S SPIRITUALITY

captive in a house ill-named "home."

The father whose proud achievements
   locked his son repeatedly
   in a prison of self-doubt.

The daughter whose marital failure
   was flung like a rock
   at her mother's divorce.

The priest whose sage counsel
   forbade his followers
   to go elsewhere.

The parishioner whose unadmitted insecurity
   found release in the denial
of the pastor's graced but all-too-human efforts.

The religious whose fear of total love
   trapped those who needed more
in the scant cell of unreasonable discipline.

Lord,
   we want to respond
   to your call that beckons us
   to read the scroll of our life's story
   honestly
   that we may set free those
   we are holding captive
by letting go of the fear that drives us
   to intimidate and force others
   to hand over their destinies to us.

Thomas R. Haney

THE DRAWING

MATT. 25:31-40   "... as you did it to the least
of these my brethren you did it
to me."

I saw a drawing the other day
  done by a second grader,
  splashed in crayon
  with a multitude of colors
which poured with careless joy
  over lines and boundaries,
  not yet inhibited by adult rules
that so often cramp the creative spirit.

It was a drawing of a little child
  pointing to a crucifix
  hanging on a boundless wall
  and underneath were the words
  scrawled in a rainbow of colors
and in an architectural carnival of sizes
    "Jesus, I love you."

I pondered the picture for quite some time
  and wondered about the way
  we educate our children.

Certainly the drawing had all the validity
  of any belief we cherish and espouse.

TODAY'S SPIRITUALITY

And yet I wondered if the teaching
　that had motivated the drawing
　did not in some way remove
　　Christ
into the past as a solitary historical figure.

We continually sing our belief,
　　"He is alive!"
　But, I wondered, have we internalized
　this belief — is he really alive for us
　　Head and Body?
Is he alive for us in those he identifies with
　in any need, small or great?

Perhaps the little second grader
　could also have been encouraged
　to draw a picture of another child
　heartbroken and crying
and the original child in the drawing
　pointing to the crying child and saying,
　　"Jesus, I love you."

Or maybe a drawing of one of those
　vague groups of indistinguishable people,
　tattered and forlorn,
　and the little child in the drawing
　pointing at them and saying,
　　"Jesus, I love you."

I wondered, too, what we adults mean
　when we pray, "Jesus, I love you."

Thomas R. Haney

You see, Christ, after all, is ever bound to us
   as Head is to the Body
   and when we pray to him
   it's never in isolation
   but all members are present
and our love should overflow
   the lines and boundaries
   of all human restrictions
creatively.

EMPOWERMENT

MARK 5:21-43   "... healing power had gone
                            out from him."

Lord,
   it had to be a humorous moment.
   Crowded in as you were, hemmed in
   by pleas for help and forgiveness,
   for love and healing,
   you wheeled around and asked,
"Who touched my clothing?"

Lord,
   I would have loved to see
   the befuddled expressions
   on your disciples' faces
   forever, it seems, contorted
   into questions and surprise.

TODAY'S SPIRITUALITY

They opened their five-loaves mouths
   and like the lawyer who asked,
   "Who is my neighbor?"
   they patronized your puzzle
   and choked back a chuckle into
   as serious a question as they could pretend,
"You're hemmed in by this crowd and you ask,
   " 'Who touched me?' "

Lord,
   your power still goes out from you
   as it did imperceptibly that day
   through the trembling fingers
   of the woman with a hemorrhage,
   as it did, quaking, to the little girl
   whose death prefigured your resurrection.

Lord,
   I, too, crowd you with my plea
   that your power straighten
   the lameness of my courage
   that I might leap
   through the halo of my dreams.

   Let your power go out and curve
   itself around my mediocrity and
   like a mist from a mount of
   transfiguration insinuate itself
   within my apathy and indifference.
   Let your power go out like
   a driving wind toppling fear,

Thomas R. Haney

like an arching flame
cauterizing anxiety and
settling as tongues of fire
on my meagerness, my measly mite.

Lord,
   let your power go out to me
   that I may leave the Eden
   of my me-and-my-God prayer,
   where I'm always putting things
   exclusively into your hands
   and refusing my responsibility
of being your co-creator.

Lord,
   I place at your disposal
   my piecemeal zeal
   my flattened ideals.
Empower me that I may empower others
   to abandon the gray sameness
   of retread solutions
   to the problem of twisting the cosmos
   into a cross to be borne on
   the shoulders of the entire race
   under the rubric of progress
   which too often is irresponsible and
uncaring exploitation of the future.
   Lord, let your power go out
   to and from me now.

150

LOVE IS RESURRECTION

JOHN 15:9-17   "Live on in my love."

Love sometimes
  is scratched
  like a tabletop
  where all the treasures
  and all the junk
  of our relationships
  have been tossed.

Love at other times
  is closed tight
  like a locket
  with a faded picture
  of someone once close
  and now barely remembered.

Love for many
  is as elusive
  as mercury:
  as soon as it is grasped
  it slips away
  and divides
  into diminished beads.

Love sometimes
  is tossed away

by those who sink
in concentric circles
of inward collapse
or forgotten in the mad rush
of angry ambition
or lost in the squeeze
of a possessive grip.

Love cannot be
without the mutuality
that draws two people
into a resurrection miracle.

At the height
of the segregation storm
parents of a first grader
sent her off for her first day
at a newly integrated school.
When school ended on that first day
the little girl's mother
met her at the door.
"How did everything go today, Honey?"
the anxious mother asked.

"Oh, Mother! You know what?
A little Negro girl sat
next to me!"
Worried that her daughter might have had
a traumatic experience
that would need explaining
the mother asked,
"And what happened, Honey?"

TODAY'S SPIRITUALITY

"We were both so scared that
all day long
we held hands."

BEING SOMEONE TO ANOTHER

JOHN 11:1-45   "And Jesus wept."

Ever since that breathtaking moment
   when clay moved and stretched
   into a luscious yawn of life
and a furtively snatched fruit
   turned glistening glory
   into sweat of the brow
   and the saliva of the death rattle
tears had been shed at gravesides.

      So one day
      the man
      who claimed
      "I am life"
      stood before
      the tomb
      of his friend
      and assaulted
      death with tears
      as heavy as
      the divine imprint
      on the original chaos.

Thomas R. Haney

So it was on another day
    a little girl was sent to the store
    with strict orders to return home
    as soon as the purchases were made.
After about an hour's delay the little girl returned
    and her anxious mother scolded
    asking where she had been.
The little girl told of how she had met her friend
    whose doll was broken
    and said she stopped to help fix it.
But, her mother reminded her, she didn't know
    how to fix a broken doll.
I know, the little girl admitted,
    so I sat with her
    and helped her to cry.

So it is that tears shed and shared
    awaken the Lazarus
    buried deep within each of us
    as sorrow turns to joy
just as once clay twitched into divine image
    and began the journey to where
    one day every tear will be wiped away.

TODAY'S SPIRITUALITY

THE FINAL RENDERING

MATT. 22:15-21   "Render to Caesar the things
                        that are Caesar's."

As you can see without
   much scrutiny
   I am wasting away.
You might say I'm on the last pages
   of the book of life.
There's no terrorism in the world
   like the word, "incurable."

You asked me how I'm holding up.
   Strange but I feel no resentment.
   My fortune is as useless
   as a one-rung ladder to heaven.
I'm as helpless as that poor peasant
   who worked for my company in Chile.
After all these years his memory haunts me
   like an unconfessed sin
   although at the time
   I hardly gave him a thought.

I remember someone wanted a policy change.
   It seems that this poor fellow in Chile
   had worked in one of my factories
   since he was 12 years old.

Thomas R. Haney

Then when he was about 54
    he fell gravely ill and was laid off.
His family asked for help from the company hospital
    but since he was no longer an employee
    he had no right to our hospital services.

The policy wasn't changed — or can I admit now
    as I stand here stripped of pretensions —
    I didn't change the policy.
He died.
    The word, "incurable," never entered
    his diagnosis.
At the time he was just one of thousands and
    thousands.
    His death didn't register a thought
    any more than a blink of my eyes.

How often I've stood here in my tower
    looking down on the streets
    where people seemed so small,
    so incidental to my empire.
You know, power doesn't corrupt,
    it tantalizes you into thinking
    you are God.
It's the God-pretension that corrupts —
    the unlearned lesson of Adam.

I've been thinking about that English ecclesiastic,
    Wolsey.
Remember the words Shakespeare put on his dying
    lips?

TODAY'S SPIRITUALITY

"Had I but served my God
with half the zeal
I serv'd my king. . . ."

I appreciate your words about an eleventh-hour
    hope.
Just remember, Father,
    when you hear all those glowing words
    about my accomplishments,
you're probably the only one I've been honest with.

ALL SAINTS DAY

MATT. 5:1-10   "Blessed are they. . . ."

They paused here
    in their transparent worldliness
they who scoff at all believers
    in the way a highwire star
    disdains a midget clown.
They paused here
    they who have no time for faith,
    here before the shrine
of a saint who had cured sickness
    with miraculous power,
paused but out of respect or curiosity
    no one knew.

Yet even those who hoist the banner
    emblazoned with the boast

Thomas R. Haney

CHRISTIAN
fail to stop or rush quickly by
   those men and women
   who endure sickness
   with miraculous patience.

We celebrate our saints
   in worship at times
   as stiff and dry
   as the plaster of paris
   our imaginations use
to visualize holy people of times past.

Still, do we celebrate those
   who feel the sting of insult
   or the slight of being ignored
but who do not grow bitter or sulk
   or retaliate
   with venomous spite?

Do we celebrate those
   who are down in health
   low in spirit
   but never despair?
Those who are brave when there's no audience
   loyal when there's no reward,
   those who fall, sometimes far,
   but rise again and push on
with sparks of new determination glinting in their
   eyes.

TODAY'S SPIRITUALITY

There are saints, aren't there,
   whose sky never
   explodes with skyrocketing bursts
   of spectacular miracles,
people whose lives are at times as dull
   and prosaic as car tracks.

   They're not canonized,
   these people,
   not saints in the formal wear
   of halos,
   these people,
   but can't we celebrate them
   if not on All Saints Day
   then on every other day?

GIFT AND TASK

MARK 4:26-34   "What comparison . . . for the
                         reign of God?"

Lord,
   you spread the word
   of your kingdom
   in stories of commonplace things
like a mustard seed
   that bursts into fullest songs
   of nested birds
like yeast kneaded into dough
   revealing the secret

159

of transformation
like the surprise of buried treasure
that opens up a world
of unlimited possibilities
and you taught us to pray,
"Thy kingdom come."

Lord,
your Church prays to this day,
"Father, all-powerful and ever-living God,
you anointed Jesus Christ
as eternal king
that he might present to you
an eternal and universal kingdom
a kingdom of truth and life
a kingdom of holiness and grace
a kingdom of justice, love and peace."

Lord,
I who am of your pilgrim people
pray for the coming of your kingdom
and yet I must ask hard questions
in my prayer.
Is yours the kingdom
which makes no deals
with the interests of those
who would have the poor
work like beasts
or who would institute
violence
in judicial systems and educational structures?

TODAY'S SPIRITUALITY

Then can I honestly pray,
"Thy kingdom come"?

Is yours the kingdom
    which abolishes all
    that turns so many people's lives
    into merchandise?
Then can I honestly pray,
"Thy kingdom come"?

Is yours the kingdom
    which assigns the land
    for the production of food
    for everyone
    and not just for exports
    which enrich those who
    already have too much
    while continuing to impoverish
    those who have nothing?
Then, Lord, tell me
    can I honestly pray,
    "Thy kingdom come"?

Lord,
    your kingdom is
    both gift and task
    both a given and a challenge.
Help us, Lord, to work
    both in the heat of the day
    and in the frenzy of the eleventh hour
for your kingdom, not ours, to come.

Thomas R. Haney

MAKING CONTACT?

MARK 10:17-22   ". . . you will then have
                                treasures in heaven."

We talk about a treasure in heaven
   to people who walk a tightrope
   over the pointed digits of a checkbook balance
and worry about the ten cent increase
   stamped indelibly on a soup can.

We talk about a treasure in heaven
   to people who sit in velvet chairs
   that haunt the boardroom table
   like judgment seats on doomsday
and who draw bottom lines into circles of poverty
   which, like lassos, bind peasants
   to plots of earth they'll never own
   'till the day they're buried.

We talk about a treasure in heaven
   to people who have no other anxiety
   than a late-running commuter train,
   who have no other desire
   than a tearful hope that husbands
   are not being unfaithful,
   who have no other goal
   than the afternoon bridge game at the club.

TODAY'S SPIRITUALITY

We talk about a treasure in heaven
   to people who keep the commandments
   in hearts like tablets of stone
   and play scrabble with gospel counsels
   which urge us to fill our hearts,
   like water jugs, with the wine of love
that the dance of life might go on and on.

Lord are we,
   with all our talk about heaven
   with all our forced divisions between
   the sacred and the profane
   with all our abstract theories
   and cliche-ridden homilies
reminiscent of pinheads and dancing angels,
   are we making contact at all
   with people where they are?

THE PRAY-ER

LUKE 21:25-28   ". . . your deliverance is near
                                 at hand."

He stumbled into the meeting
   out of the nowhere where
   so many exist.
   A gaunt, apocalyptic-looking man,
   more than a little tipsy.

Thomas R. Haney

The members of the prayer group
  were, to say the least, taken aback.
They smiled a smile of embarrassment,
  whether for him or themselves
  they couldn't be sure.

He sat and sighed a mutter —
  or was it a prayer?
  The group was too shocked to know,
  some were scandalized, others
bewildered
  but they took to their joy of praying
  and watched the man out of the corners
  of their fleeting glances.

Suddenly the unknown figure
  who had appeared wistfully
  from his edge of the world to theirs
  (the Spirit still blows where it will)
  opened his mouth and spoke
  as though in slow motion:
"Let's say a prayer.
  Close your eyes and picture
  a black man with no lips and no legs.
  He wants to sing but he has no lips.
  He wants to dance but he has no legs.
  Amen."

In a slurred, fuzzy moment
  he rose, and bobbing and weaving,
  left the group to their prayer
  and to their astonishment.

164

TODAY'S SPIRITUALITY

Lord,
    all judgment is yours
    and you alone read hearts.
In our deepest prayer, if it is real,
    we accept others as you send them
    and judge them not
lest the deliverance you send through them
    be lost forever to our prayer.

STRUGGLE FOR HELP

JOHN 17:24-26   "... that they also ... may
                          be with me ..."

He called
again
for help.

I thought it was all forgotten,
slipped into the spaces
between the dates, then and now,
but spaces often bulge
    with memories thought dismissed.

He calls
again
for help.

I repeat to him my
    borrowed wisdom:

Thomas R. Haney

Put it all behind you.
Get on with your life.
Let bygones be bygones.
Trust in God —
    words that soothe all
    but those who had been there.

Now I heard he stabbed
    his brother the other night
    and strolled naked
    except for the dripping knife
    down the midnight boulevard.

In fact, we'll never forget
    the wasted blood of Vietnam
    while one memory is a nightmare
    while one veteran slips into the spaces
    between the dates of then and now.

He'll call
again
for help.
    I'm sure.

THE GIFT OF DOUBT

JOHN 20:19-31   "... be not unbelieving,
                              but believing."

I need the silence of Thomas' doubt.
    I need a week to juggle the words,

TODAY'S SPIRITUALITY

"He is risen!"
in rhythmic concentration.

I need to feel part of the group again
  to be reconciled
  to come to grips with wounds
  I have never touched.
I need to challenge faith, to grab it
  until it coughs up mystery
to know I can believe even though I do not see
  to utter my surrender,
  "My Lord and my God,"
  and feel the warmth of the Breath
  that forms us into one Body.

I need the freedom of Thomas' doubt
  to ask my question,
"Where is your resurrection power,
  reconciling us, making us one?"

Where is this power in the bitter divorce
  shattering lives and loves
  down the street in that cozy home?
And what about that brutal beating
  the old vagrant suffered
  at the fists of uncaring hoodlums?

Where is this power in the bloody strife,
  the murdered brothers and sisters of Abel,
  in Northern Ireland, in South Africa,
  in Central America, in so many places?

Thomas R. Haney

And what about the casual termination of life
   in wombs created in God's image?

What about that married couple kneeling
   so fervently there in church
   and barely speaking to each other
   the rest of the week?
Where is the resurrection power
   among those plundered peasants
   whose sweaty backs serve
   as pedestals to elevate
   the comfort of our lifestyles?

And what about the unadmitted violence
   seething within my own heart
   erupting through my private piety
into public words of fury and gestures of vengeance?

I need the break of Thomas' doubt
   to reformulate my question,
   asking no longer, never again,
"Where is your resurrection power?"
   but probing our own reality,
"Why do we not receive what is being offered,
   the power of your resurrection?"

WINDOWED WISDOM

JOHN 17:9-19   ". . . but these are in the
world . . ."

When I was a child
   the greatest adventure of all
   was to take my eyes
   to the corner grocery store
and let them roam around
   the Eden of the candy counter.

As I grew older candy gave way
   to books and such
and like my chocolate-filled eyes
   of forgotten times past
   my mind scurried from
   one printed oasis to another.

It was and is, I tell myself, a search
   for the sweet wisdom that cracks open
   the universe of reality
where angels give way to ponderous theories
and novenas slip off to make room
   for a mature approach to a primordial God.

Yet now I realize that
   I've been flying high

Thomas R. Haney

over mountains of hardcover ideas
as if in a low-flying jet from which
   I can see all and yet nothing at all.

How long it takes for us to land,
   to settle out of the blur
   of a twisted search
and walk slowly through the thickets
of overgrown epigrams and tombstone jargon
until we can sit on a grassy patch
   of revealed insights.

In the jungle of buzz words and doublespeak
   of gossip and inanities
   a vine of life-giving words grows
on which we can swing close to earth
   and up into the highest heaven:
". . . not to be served but to serve."

Lord, why do we bypass
   windowed wisdom
in search of dusty esoteric knowledge?
Is it because we live in our heads
   and fear that the wisdom of the Garden God
   will force a change in the way we live
in the body of our world?

THE DESERT OF LENT

MARK 1:12-15   "The Spirit sent Jesus out
toward the desert."

"And what do you want to find
  in this desert?" asked the old nun.
"Total detachment from the world,"
  answered the young novice.
"Ah," sighed the old nun, "and will you
  also detach yourself from humor?"
"I don't understand . . ." hesitated the young
  novice.

"Here in this desert we call Lent,
  my child, we leave behind
  that which we will later come
  to appreciate all the more.
Without humor, I'm afraid, detachment
  is a mirage for a barren hatred
  of the world and penance twists
into an angry need for harsh self-punishment.

"Study the stories Jesus told.
  A wise mystic, he used humor
  to shock his audience into truth.

When he shook the desert sands from the folds
  of fasting and temptation, he emerged,

171

Thomas R. Haney

able to proclaim the time of fulfillment
because he had not left his humor behind
before or after his desert experience.''

"Does fulfillment include
a deeper appreciation of the world, then?''
asked the young novice.

"Can we relish the higher things of God
if we cannot enjoy
the simple things that come along
as his ordinary gifts?''
asked the old nun in return.

"When Jesus left the desert,
did he not also preach reform?''
asked the young novice.

"Indeed he did, my child,''
replied the old nun.
"And the reform of the desert experience
we call Lent
can lead us from a world-hating self
to a passionate love of the world
in all its God-given possibilities
for nobility and graciousness.''

"To follow Christ into the desert, then,
means that we engage the world
in its struggle for nobility
and spend ourselves in this quest,''
observed the young novice.

TODAY'S SPIRITUALITY

"Yes, my child," the old nun agreed,
    "and the desert we call Lent
    gives us distance and time
    to see with wilderness clarity
    the possibilities of the world
    and the energy to confront it
    with the beauty of the risen Lord."

"And shock it into the truth
    of its possibilities
    with his humor?"
    the young novice smiled.

SUBVERTED ASSUMPTIONS

LUKE 10:25-37   "There was a man going
                       down. . . ."

Jesus wrapped the world
    with his stories
    and tied the stories together
with a timeless ribbon so that today we can still
    open his gift
    and discover surprises
    beyond our staid expectations.

The stories Jesus told
    pulled the rug from under
the comfortable assumptions of those who sought
    easy answers

173

and hoped for confirmation
of their favorite conclusions.

It's as though Jesus' challenge
   went something like this:
Your assumption is that your priests
   are concerned, involved men,
   caring for those in need giving leadership
   in ways of loving service.
   Right?

Let me tell you a story.
   And soon his listeners were
   transported to a road from
   Jerusalem to Jericho.
   Once there was a traveler.
Thieves beat, robbed and left him to die
   in a ditch.

Now it happened that a priest was passing by that
   ditch
   and that's just what he did —
   passed by.
Which of the passersby was neighbor
   to the traveler in the ditch?
   Despite their assumption
   no one in the crowd
   could answer, "The priest."

His stories still work
still turn our assumptions
upside down.

TODAY'S SPIRITUALITY

We listen to this story and react
  with the typical assumption,
    "I would have stopped."

And the story challenges us on this day
  of hearing
  to examine our assumption:

  Who is in my ditch?
What if it's someone who hates me,
  who has betrayed a confidence,
  who has ruined my reputation,
  hurt me beyond repair (I think),
who has tramped on me to fulfill his ambition,
  how does my assumption hold up?
  Stop or pass by?

  Who is in my ditch?
What if it's someone who preaches what
  I don't want to hear,
  or someone who criticizes affluence
  and makes me face my selfishness,
  or someone who advocates peacemaking
  and challenges my militarism.
  Would I still stop at my ditch?

Is my assumption ever open
  to the Storyteller's conclusion,
"Whatsoever you do to one of these . . . you do
  to me"?

Thomas R. Haney

THE CHALLENGE

JOHN 15:1-8   "I am the Vine."

He was always doing this, especially
   when they thought they had him
   squeezed comfortably onto
   the tablets of their understanding.

He'd walk the dusty roads of Palestine
   rub elbows with anybody and everybody
   in the crowded streets of Jerusalem
   wend his way over mountains brought low
   through valleys that had been filled
   across crooked ways he left straight
   by rough ways he trampled smooth
and then finally he'd look at fellow pilgrims and
   say,
   "I am the way."

He'd enter a synagogue on the Sabbath,
   unroll the scroll of law and order
   and describe a seventy-times-seven God
   and tell stories like the one about the father
   who rushed down into ragged sin
   with a cloak, sandals and a ring
   and pulled sonship out of guilt
and then finally he'd look at the startled faces and

176

TODAY'S SPIRITUALITY

whisper,
"I am the truth."

He'd close the door of his carpenter shop
   shake the sawdust from his sandals
   and go for a walk on the hillside
   among the lilies and ripe harvest.
Then he'd stop and watch shepherds
   calling all the sheep by name
   in a voice known only to each,
   and observe a ewe lamb scramble off
   to test the stamina of a searching shepherd
and then finally he'd smile at the villagers and say,
   "I am the sheepgate."

He'd sit in the shade of grape arbor
   inhaling the sweet scent of
   ripening grapes
   and think of wine and a final meal
   where covenant would be sealed in blood
   and shudder at the prospect of a chalice
   that would not pass
and then finally he'd look at his closest and
   announce,
   "I am the vine."

Just as when he said, "I am the way"
   he implied, "Come, follow me,"
   or when he said, "I am the truth,"
   he meant that they would be set free
   or when he said, "I am the sheepgate,"

Thomas R. Haney

the promise was that ninety-nine
would be left for one,
so when he announced, "I am the vine,"
there could be no doubt
that those who believed
would know they had to be the branches.

GRATITUDE

LUKE 17:11-19   "Where are the other nine?"

"P-L-E-A-S-E," she mimicked,
her five-year-old teeth bared
like the blades of a blender
not in defiance but in a challenge:
to see how much she could get away with.

"Thank you," her mother corrected later
and through lips encased
in half-eaten potatoes and peas
the little student heaved a hefty sigh
of chagrin and surrender
and mumbled a desperate almost inaudible
"T-h-a-n-k y-o-u."

Manners aren't as spontaneous
as teary-eyed tantrums.
They're learned through the monotony
of exasperating repetition
and often forgotten like dates
after a history test.

TODAY'S SPIRITUALITY

We enter the Jesus story.
"Were not all ten made clean?"
We feel his born again exclusion
of being taken for granted.
It's the crowded inn all over again.
And we know that nine
times out of ten we fail to return
and give thanks.

The nine bound by the Law
were too scrupulous fulfilling
the letter of the Law,
too busy showing off their
cleanliness-next-to-Godliness cure
to scrutinizing priests
who had to admit
that a carpenter's word could smoothe
the lepers' sores
like his plane could shave wood.
And so the nine never bothered to return,
never bothered to say "Thank you."

Within the Jesus story we know
how big our "Please" is,
how tiny, almost inaudible,
our "Thank you."

We storm your door at midnight, Lord,
after you've retired from our pleas,
begging you for more —
bread and some wine
and an altar of sorts

Thomas R. Haney

is all we want, all we say we need
   for now.

Then by some sudden transposition
   we are inside the house
   behind the midnight door
and you are outside knocking, banging,
   asking us for Eucharist
      for thanksgiving.
That's all you want, all you need for now.

THE PRIORITY OF HUMOR

MARK 9:30-37   ". . . they had been arguing
                     about who was the most
                     important."

The squabbles were as intense
   as a child's innocence
   as frequent as an adolescent's doubts
   as wearying as an adult's regrets.

"Who is the most important?"
"Who will sit on the right,
   one on the left of Power
   when the Kingdom opens up
   like a banquet hall where
   the first shall be last and
the most powerful will wait on tables?"

180

TODAY'S SPIRITUALITY

The disciples —
   so serious, so intense
   about themselves
   that they missed the point
   when the Word cracked like a joke
   and reversed their priorities.

If they had a sense of humor
   they would have filled the Kingdom
   with laughter when they saw his point
   that the position of power
   was the prestige of being last,
   that the aura of authority
   was the glory of being a servant,
that the most important was the least.

But no!
They were so busy arguing among themselves
   about their importance to God
   about their indispensability
to his plan that they missed his point.

So Jesus entered their humorless
   arguments and told them a joke
   about indispensability:
"There was this wealthy farmer
   who built even bigger and better barns
   and then heaved a final sigh of relief
   on the deathbed of self-sufficiency."
The disciples didn't laugh —
   they had missed the point.
"Teacher, what does this parable mean?"

Thomas R. Haney

Have you ever noticed
  how laughter gets buried
  like a miser's hoard
  deep inside the vaults of our hearts
  whenever we feel indispensable
  whenever we get so involved
  in our cause or in our movement
that we miss the point of our own commitment?

Have you ever noticed that
  humor, laughter, even joy
  belong to those who have made
  peace with their own mortality,
who know as surely as they know
  their morning coffee's too hot
  to drink but still needs more sugar
that when they're gone
  the world will go on and get along?

So the humorous squeeze each second for all its life
  and fill each moment with all their growth
  and laugh at the cosmic joke
  of ebbtides and empty nests
and of people who are as necessary
  as branches for a vine
yet as dispensable as a martyr's zeal,
  a prophet's voice, a savior's tomb.

TODAY'S SPIRITUALITY

TWO KINDS OF BARNS

LUKE 12:16-21   "I will pull down my barns
                                 and build larger ones . . ."

Bigger and better barns.
  Our lives swell
  with plans for them
like my search for words
  that can be stored away for posterity,
or your fantasies about a love,
  always flawless, never faltering.

Bigger and better barns
  stuffed with dreams,
bulging with selfish security
  or smug immortality.

Bigger and better barns
  in which our ambition,
  like the widow's mite,
  waits humbly disguised as zeal
for the abundant blessings
  of promotion and advancement.

Bigger and better barns
  hoarding in gleaming vaults
  affluent profits from grain sales
while 40,000 human beings

183

die each day from
malnutrition and starvation.

Bigger and better barns
    carved into pentagonal silos,
    housing weapons,
    failsafe for their inventors
    doomsday for their victims
    push-button for their managers
and we have met the victims
    and they are us.

Bigger and better barns
    safeguards against a hope
    that keeps our minds off
    the immediate, day-to-day
    task of survival.
A hope too dangerous to be practical.

Smaller and older barns
    never quite filled
    always open
where caring and sharing
    are multiplied
    like loaves and fishes
and service is often nailed
    to the cross of human suffering
only to rise to the joy
    of greater prodigality.

MISPLACED PEACE

JOHN 14:23-29   ". . . my peace is my
                                       gift to you."

The news reports ache
  like calluses on our feet
  like an abscessed tooth
  like daggers thrust into our sinews.
Reports of killings and preparations for more
  of hope invested in armaments
and we sit tentatively with His promise that
  He gives peace not as the world gives it.

We scurry past his words as if they were
  an overfamiliar landscape
without ever asking,
  "How does the world give peace?"

  How?
as an interruption of wars
as a tiny beachhead off from the ocean of blood
as a brave lad who died for his country
as a ceaseless tear shed silently in a parental bed
as a clamorous throng celebrating armistice
as a brave obituary of the last surviving veteran
as a punctuation mark in the endless paragraph of
    hatred
as a fireworks display on a holiday anniversary

185

Thomas R. Haney

as a wave of crosses blurred white in Arlington
    Cemetery.

    How comfortable it is for us, how peaceful,
    to be distracted by our busyness
    while the host is being offered on the paten
    for the violence throughout the world.
When will we offer, with the intensity of a mystic,
    the world's violence
    on the paten of massacred masses
in broad daylights, as high noon, in blazing sun —
    the moment of crucifixion?

    When will we stop hiding out in sacred places
        within the walls of our churches
        rapt in silent adoration of a God
who lives among His people?
        And when will we stop
        carrying that same silence out
into the killings of God's people
        without uttering a single protest?

We who are so comfortable, self-satisfied,
    defensive, saved, peaceful
    because the world blesses us with its
"Peace be with you"?

When?
    When we start trying to absorb
    the beliefs we cherish, even hoard,
in our churches,
    when we carry those beliefs

TODAY'S SPIRITUALITY

quickly, intently, brazenly into the streets
like the early Christians who carried fragments
   from the community worship
   to those about to die for their beliefs,
when we start taking people seriously
   in their vulnerability
   so that we know we're taking God seriously,
when what we do in our churches
   becomes a protest against
the maimings, the killings, the exploitings
   that smooth injustices provoke,
when what we do in our worship makes us
   human enough to care.
Then will we have chosen peace as He gives it,
   peace as His gift.

A PRAYER FOR DIVERSITY

JOHN 17:11-19   ". . . that they may be one,
                         even as we are one."

Ponder, Lord, our disarray
   as you hear our prayers
   for unity
   rising out of the crushed bones
   of our loveless encounters
   (often in your name)
and know that your Son's prayer
   that we all might be one
   waits,

Thomas R. Haney

like a dry eye for a tear,
to be fulfilled.

Lord, indweller of my being,
how often do we gather
to break bread
and tell the story
of your oneness with your Son,
yet leave only with our own brokenness
to reenter lives torn and fragmented by hostility?

Lord, closer to me than I am to myself,
look at the way we fool ourselves
pretending to unite
under the banner of defense,
refusing to admit that defensiveness
springs from fear and suspicion
and ends in faster missiles and bigger bombs.

There are times, Jesus, my friend,
when I want to enter
into your prayer for unity
especially when I am feeling
disgruntled or disillusioned
with my fellow members of your Body
while conveniently forgetting
my own sins which agitate,
even horrify,
those who annoy me with their foibles and quirks.

There are times, Lord, indweller of my life —
many more than I care to count —

TODAY'S SPIRITUALITY

when my prayer for unity
is but the lip service I pay
to the formality of rushed prayer
and mindless rites.

Thrust my prayer back at me, Lord,
dwelling within my becoming,
push it down into the depths
of my heart where I have compromised
and accommodated ever so comfortably
to serving you and the mammon of power
while professing my distance from the world's
   values.

When we pray for unity, indwelling Lord,
   let us see the crevices
   of our divisiveness.
   Let us feel the pain
   of our self-righteous judgments.
   Let us laugh at our fears
   until we allow for diversity
within our unity.

EMMAUS JOURNEYS

LUKE 24:13-35   ". . . they recognized him in
                       the breaking of the bread."

What begins as a journey
   of distress, disappointment
and doubt

turns into an adventure
of trust, faith and burning response.

We all have our Emmaus journeys.
  Journeys of personal prayerful probings
  where we wrestle to make sense
  of the life-giving insights of the Word
in a world going mad with indifference and hostility.

Why do the innocent suffer?
Why are so many deprived of the bare necessities?
Why the hi-tech slaughter?
  How can any of this make sense?
Why is greed rewarded with ruthless power?
Why is the disregard for life prized?
  We walk along struggling with the problems,
  trying our heartiest to listen to the Word.

The Emmaus road is no freeway.

Then the Word tells us a story
  about another journey
  from Jerusalem to Jericho.
You, he tells us, make this journey
  each day of your lives.
As you make your way, you see
  the innocent exploited
  the deprived ignored
  the murdered unavenged
    the greedy rewarded
    the killers supported

TODAY'S SPIRITUALITY

and you must decide whether or not
  you will stop.

If you stop
  you may find answers
  to your questions.

The story ends
  and we know that the answers
  will not come from theory
but through encounter with our
  Emmaus companion
  as he challenges us
  on the way to Jericho
in the persons of those in need,
  in need of physical assistance
  in need of moral guidance.

In those with whom we must break
  the bread of our lives
  as surely as we share Eucharist
for it is in the breaking and the sharing
  that we will recognize
  our companion, our guest
who has become our host.

Thomas R. Haney

MISSION

LUKE 10:1-9   "The Lord . . . sent them
in pairs. . . ."

Roads of clay
  roads of new life.
Go down those roads two by two,
  and tell the story to other
  Adams and Eves
of the divine possibilities of being human.

Go down the roads of centuries,
  seventy-two disciples times millions
and tell the story to other Magdalenes
  and Peters and Judases
of the divine reach of human forgiveness,
  the new incarnation
  of a returning Prodigal,
  the eternal scandal
  of a Zacchaeus perched on a tree of life.

"Come down," he had said
  and Zacchaeus did
  what he himself would never do —
  he came down from his tree —
it's the difference between
  giving and receiving
  saving and being saved.

TODAY'S SPIRITUALITY

And the tree's roots stretched back
   beyond human memory into
   primitive fantasy where the Garden God
   preserved the secret of good and evil
until the hour had come and the Son of Man
   was glorified on a tree
   where good publicized evil
   and became the fruit of the vine
until the end of time, until the eternal Now.

But for now go two by two
   in the highways and byways
   and tell the story of a peace
   the world cannot give
   that turns the world upside down,
   a peace that dethrones the mighty
   and exalts the lowly.

Don't be anxious about what
   you shall wear or eat
   about walking staffs or sandals.
   about frustration and burn-out.
Put your hand to the plough,
   the harvest will be rich
   and the laborers few.
Sufficient for the day is the trouble therein.

Then come aside and rest awhile
   The triumphs will always be
   those of the Cross,
   the victories out of apparent failures.
I want nothing to be wasted.

Thomas R. Haney

It's not the accomplishment,
  but the pursuit,
  not the labor but the zeal,
  not the law but the Spirit,
  not the baptism but the life,
  not the merits but the hope,
until the end of time, until the eternal Now.

NOT TIME BUT INTENSITY

LUKE 2:21-24   "... the name of Jesus was given
           the child. ...."

I looked at my calendar
  lying on my desk
  like a microchip of eternity.
As I glanced over the coming months
  a thought flashed like a spotlight,
"Will one of those months claim me
  from these fleeting moments called life?"

It was not a morbid thought and
  its impact fled me like an escaped prisoner.
It was more like a traffic light
  signaling me to stop and
  asking for no interpretation.

The months ahead
  reminded me
  of the years gone by

194

TODAY'S SPIRITUALITY

which had been torn away
   like pieces of protective tile
   snapping off a space shuttle
   leaving me ever more vulnerable
to the death rays of the lifegiving sun.

In this vulnerable mood
   I entered the Temple story
   where the Cave Child
   was being offered
as the Lamb of sacrifice
   where the carpenter's son
   was being hammered together
as the Altar of the living temple
   where the sign of contradiction
   was being raised
as the High Priest of the new covenant.

I asked the Mother who was pondering
   in her heart
   the sword that would pierce her soul,
"Is this 'he who is to come'?
   Will the lame dance the light fantastic?
   Will the blind etch immortal art?
   Will the deaf sing arias with perfect pitch?
Will he lay down his life of his own accord?"

Then I heard the name being given the child:
   Jesus
and I knew it was he who had come
   to save his people from their sins.

Thomas R. Haney

As I returned from the Temple story
  I also knew
  that it didn't really matter
  which month might claim me
eventually
  as long as I laid down my life
daily
  as a sacrifice for the sins
  that immobilize the oppressed
  and dehumanize the poor
  whether in spirit or in flesh.

Life, I now realized, was not measured
  in terms of length of days
  or months on a calendar
but in the intensity of the self-oblation.

THE SOCIAL GOSPEL

LUKE 14:7-14   ". . . do not invite your friends
                              or brothers or relations or
                              wealthy neighbors."

Do we approach the words of Jesus
  with the literalism of a hospital ward:
  the lame, the crippled, the blind?
These and only these to be invited
  within the begging circle of our celebration?
Are these remnants of human destitution
  stereotypes of the gospel

196

TODAY'S SPIRITUALITY

kept at the comfortable distance of centuries
   between sacred writ and secular newsprint?

Or are the beggars, the lame, the crippled, the blind
   merely the beginning of our universal concern?
Are they not the gospeled glimpses
   of the oppressed, the imprisoned, the starving,
   the tortured, the marginalized of our day?
Those swatted to death by the single swing
   of the arm of authoritarian militarism?
Those enslaved by multinational profiteers?

"Hey! This is the gospel!
   Not some treatise on sociology.
   We read it to find out how to save our souls
   not to map out political strategies."

But doesn't the gospel today include
   those whose brittle bones of pride
   have been smashed in an unjust cell
   into the cringing crawl of a political cripple?
Or those whose vision of hope
   has been scorched into blindness
   with a lit cigarette in a torture chamber?

"Hey! We provide crutches for the crippled
   and seeing-eye dogs for the blind
   and soup kitchens for the poor beggars.
These others you talk about
   are the burden of governments
   not the business of saving souls!"

Thomas R. Haney

And so it goes.
　　Those in the front seats
　　seldom turn around
　　seldom look back at those
　　standing in the rear with no seats
those most desperately in need.

But the marvel is that it's
　　never too late.
The challenge is always there
　　to bring those in the back
　　up to the front
and never ask for thanks.

THE GIFT OF BEAUTY

MATT. 11:2-11　　　　　"What did you go out to the
　　　　　　　　　　　wasteland to see . . .?"

Beauty is ultimate, the artist
　　proclaimed in her lecture,
　　her words dripping multicolored
　　insights on the canvas
　　of our expectations.

The contrast of pain and joy,
　　of loss and ecstasy,
　　of tragedy and harmony,
these, she exclaimed, are the
　　darkness and light

TODAY'S SPIRITUALITY

of art, lived and created.
It is the wholeness we call beauty.

Later, as I pondered the Baptist,
   his life of contrast and harmony,
   I recalled the artist's words.

The dark calls for conversion
   in fact the light the love
   the pink of creating out of
   the orange of desolation,
   the oozing purple of sin admitted,
   the sparkling yellow of conversion,
   the sprightly opal of serenity.

The Baptist, I finally realized, was
   beautiful
   because he was shareable.
Not a prophet who confirmed the worst
   fears people had about themselves
but a prophet who followed the footprints of God
   in the stories of those who told them
   and who shared Mystery through them.

Beauty revels in unity:
   the steadfast star with
   puncturing enlightenment,
   the angelic song, rhythmic
   syllables of swaying revelation,
   shepherds, shrugging shoulders
   of doubt and credence,
   on a trek of predicted discovery,

all fuse in the person of this prophet
   whose pointed words pierced
   Mystery even though but for an instant,
"Behold the Lamb of God."

Beauty heightens the cosmic glory
   when we recognize
   we are all born for the altar.
Each child of us a lamb of God.

We burst breathless out of the
   red river of baptismal sacrifice,
   cleansed for the glistening altar
   where beauty is the harmony
of living for and laying down our lives
   for the Lamb
   identified even with the least.

A SCRUPLE OF UNWORTHINESS

JOHN 1:29-34   "Look there! The Lamb
                        of God. . . ."

Stark as the Lamb's altar
as intimidating as long lines
   of goats separated from sheep
with warnings snapping from his lips
   like a brood of vipers
John the Baptist
   stands at the edge

200

TODAY'S SPIRITUALITY

of a new era
pointing us to the Lamb of God.

The priest enjoyed jotting down notes like these
    for his homilies
    far more than preaching them.
Here alone with his notepad and words
    he had control.

His thoughts wandered as they often did,
    and settled, like a twister
    blasting the calm of his mood,
    on the encounter with a woman
whose piety had become his perplexity.

"I can't drink from the cup," she had said,
    planting her conviction firmly
    in the mystery of Godhead,
"I just don't feel worthy."

His first impulse was to slash through
    her pious protestation
    with the razor-sharp remark,
    "That's illogical!"

    He backed off.
    Was he not a teacher?
    Explanation not condemnation
    was the proper response.

"We believe," he spoke slowly
    as though to a first communicant,

Thomas R. Haney

"that Jesus is present, body and blood
  soul and divinity under
  the appearance of bread, don't we?"
She nodded her head affirmatively, wistfully.

"Well," he continued, "he is present
  in the same way
  under the appearance of wine.
So if you feel worthy enough to receive
  the consecrated host,
there's no difference in drinking from the cup."

"You see," he spoke with persuasive patience,
  "Jesus is the sacrificial Lamb
  who laid down his life for his friends.
  He wants us to be comfortable
  with him, to be his friends.
Okay?"

"Okay," she answered more
out of respect than conviction.

"But I still can't gaze
at the host during the
consecration like you tell us to.
I just feel too unworthy."

He returned to his notes
  on John the prophet.
  He felt more comfortable
more in control when writing his notes

than when playing the role
of teacher.

DWELLING PLACES

JOHN 1:35-42   "Where do you dwell?"

The Baptist who dined on
    grasshoppers and wild honey
    still had an eye for
    a Lamb that was food from heaven.

But He who trailed the smell of banquet
    set a table of invitation
with bread broken and wine spilled
    and those who sought the last places
    would be moved up into the sanctuary
    where the host became the meal
    and the guests became the host.

The Baptist stood alone near the waters
    of sorrow and repentance
    as his followers caught up
    with the Lamb and asked,
    "Where do you dwell?"

The Lamb turned toward his destiny
    like a man who put his
    hand to the plough,
    "Come and you will see."

203

Thomas R. Haney

They followed with the echo
  of their question
  still throbbing in their hearts,
  "Where do you dwell?"

Among stones that look like bread
  but smell like desert,
  among loaves too few
  but feeding thousands
upon the grassy knoll of infinite bounty.

  "Where do you dwell?"
Among wheat fields white for harvest
  but bleak with laborers too few.
On temple tops and mountain peaks
  with knees too loyal to bend
  to the promises of prestige and power
spawned by the Prince of Darkness
  whose realm is webbed with lies.

  "Where do you dwell?"
Among tax collectors and prostitutes
  embarrassments to the
  rigidly religious
  who prize propriety above reality
  and hurl stones of judgment
  against lives feebly stirring with grace.

In precious ointment and repentant tears
  that bathe the feet
that will not cease in the chase of saving love.

TODAY'S SPIRITUALITY

And now the Lamb, the pursued turned pursuer,
   turns the question on me,
   a pleasant pilgrim through the story,
    "Where do *you* dwell?"

I have dwelt on cushions of convenience
   and within the confines of indifference
   but lately I have been dwelling
   in the image of a child,
     skin threadbare
     stomach bloated
     eyes hollow
open sores eating away at what's left
   of his flesh
starving
   diseased
     wasted
discarded on the wayside of human concern
   helpless
     innocent
       dying.

And, Lord, Lamb of God,
    I hate
      the petty obsessions
      of the pitifully self-centered
including
my own.

Thomas R. Haney

THE ADVENT WREATH OF SPINACH

MARK 13:33-37   "You do not know when the
appointed time will come."

If you're like me
  you'll remember
  the maternal motivation
  at dinner table
where steaming spinach sat untouched.

"Look at Popeye," Mother would urge
  as though the words themselves
  were some magical incantation
  seducing the image of a mountainous bicep
to pop into mind just as Popeye's arm popped a
  muscle.

You'll remember too that spinach wasn't
  the only thing on the menu of growing up.
"Don't forget to say your prayers," Mother'd call
  out
  as you were yawning yourself to bed.
"When's the last time you were at confession?"
  she'd say as you were getting ready
to trade your dime for a Saturday afternoon at the
  movies.
  Why was everything that was good for you
    like spinach?

TODAY'S SPIRITUALITY

Yet we know that muscles don't just pop up
   any more than we'll wake up in heaven
   one day and wonder how on earth we got there.

All that mothers wanted was for us to grow up big
   and strong
   and it never dawned on us then
   that one day we would grow
through big and strong to small and weak
   and that all the spinach in the world
would not forestall the ultimate smallness and
   weakness
   we call Death.

Perhaps the only real answer to the question,
   "What're you going to be when you grow up?"
   is, "Somebody who's dying sooner."

Not that we are to stand on the edge of life
   frozen in fear or shaking with anxiety
   as the alien shuttle of death and judgment
   slowly docks on the space station Earth.
No, because through death we will continue
   to grow big and strong.

Waiting for death is our New Testament way
   of looking forward to the coming of the Messiah.

We live in a dragged-out Advent
   but an advantageous Advent too
for even though we can't pinpoint the moment of

death
we know the event's for sure.

Death will come
  as sure as our Advent will end
  as sure as the Messiah will return
  as sure as the next harvest of spinach
  but it'll be no more distasteful
  than finally conceding
  (who'd ever have guessed it?)
  that today I revel in spinach salad
  (smothered with hot bacon dressing, of course).

EVEN THE LEAST

JOHN 1:35-42   "We have found the Messiah!"

The old man, whose tattered
  shoes made tiny molehill
  mounds in the snow which
  reached up and plugged the holes
  in the soles of those tattered shoes
  until the next step,
moved stealthily like a crouched lion
  on a cold mountain of hostile predators
  from his heating grate
  to his morning garbage can.

A few weeks back he had found
  a treasure in his garbage can.

TODAY'S SPIRITUALITY

A worn and shabby Christmas wreath
which he carried with him
until it fell apart
much as did his youthful dreams
so many years back.

In his world of macadam logic
where he faded from the conscience
of a society which celebrated
neat and forgettable niches
like "street people,"
everything seemed to fall apart,
and everyone, too.

His Christmas gift again this year
had been the Gothic church which
was open a few hours
before and after midnight
at this one time each year.
There behind an ornate column
he sat near a real radiator
and this time
no one told him he had to leave.

The preacher had said something
that puzzled him still.
The old man's worn neurons, whose
electric arcs of insight
cast but a dim glimmer
of intuition in the hallway of his brain,
had created many such puzzles of late.

Thomas R. Haney

The preacher had said that if Mary had been filled
  with reason, she'd never have been
  filled with child
and that all of us should have her faith
  to receive everyone as Christ
  the Messiah.

In the warm bustle of the exit
  from the heated church
  the old man had come up abruptly
  to face a frail, bearded young man.
In the twinkling lights that darkened
  the street into a blur of phantoms,
the frail, bearded young man had handed
  him a blanket and a five-dollar bill.

The old man had blinked and stammered,
  "Are you the Messiah?"
"No," the frail, bearded young man
  had answered,
  "but at this hour
  on this Christmas morning
I believe I have found the Messiah."

TODAY'S SPIRITUALITY

A CHRISTMAS STORY

MATT. 11:2-11   "Go and tell John what you
                       hear and see. . . ."

Standing in line at the counter
    amid the bundles of Christmas shoppers
    I had time to stare.

The old man was sitting in a chair
    over by the door, waiting,
leaning on his gnarled, knotty cane,
    his face etched in the deepest
    darkest midnight frown,
lines of age or scars of disgruntled anger?
    (I remember thinking how
    his gloomy stare into nowhere
    contrasted so with the dancing
    Christmas glitter throughout the store.)

Whatever, the grooves of his frowning face
    looked as permanent and immovable
    as if carved in granite.

A young mother came bustling through
    the door with two little boys
    being hauled on either hand.

Thomas R. Haney

The smaller one, about one and a half years old,
   charged into the store
   like a whirlwind or sheer excitement
   chattering like a flock of magpies.

Like a magnetic needle he sprang right to the old
   man
   talking in a language
   describable only as gibberish
   (although what he was saying
   obviously meant something to him).
   He pushed his little forefinger
   against the old man's crooked cane
   probing with jinglebell curiosity
   a mystery known to himself alone.

Suddenly the old man's face, which only moments
   before was a great jagged stone
   of somber detachment,
   burst, like a shining star,
   into the most marvelous, magnetic,
   broadest, most beautiful smile
I had ever seen.

The young mother apologized distractedly
   and pulled her little boys
deep into the Christmas-wrapped store.

The old man sat there wreathed in his smile
   as though his whole personality
   had come fully alive.

TODAY'S SPIRITUALITY

As I passed him on my way out
   he looked up at me,
   "Merry Christmas!" he called out.
   I felt alive.

A GRANDNIECE'S CHRISTMAS GIFT

LUKE 3:10-18   "What ought we to do?"

Remind me, Linda, someday
   to tell you, when many Christmases
   have become incarnate in your
   experience of a God who so loved
   the world that he sent his only Son,
about the Christmas day you unwittingly
   taught me a most significant,
   most sacramental lesson.

Remind me to tell you about the Christmas
   when the lights on the tree were
   like stars so close you were able
   to stretch up and touch them
   and, with a squeal of glee, show us,
   with the intuition of a two-year-old
   that Happiness was withn the reach
   of any-year-old.

Remind me to tell you
   how you tiptoed ever so errantly
   in and around and sometimes through

213

Thomas R. Haney

the merrily wrapped Christmas gifts
strewn in piles of loving generosity
all over the living room floor.

And how you stopped at certain intervals
and within a twinkling of an eye,
like a jolly little elf busily
intent in a Christmas wonderland,
you stooped to a multicolored package
and ever so gently tore off the tissue
that hid the treasures of Christmas delights.

Remind me to tell you
how you stood erect as a Christmas tree
and in a triumphant tone like that of
those angels who first rocked
the manger with their Glorias,
you sighed aloud with amazement
and wonder a long, soft, gleeful
"Oooooohhh."

Then you hurried off, oblivious
of all the adult eyes playfully
laughing at your Christmas antics,
in search of another surprise wrapped
and waiting for your Christmas fingers.

Remind me to tell you, Linda — for herein
is the lesson you taught me —
how you hurried off with
green and red streamers trailing

after you without your ever once
opening the boxed gifts.

Even today I still pray out of your experience
and realize with greater depth than then
how I, too, hurry off to busy details
without ever opening the prodigal gifts
lavished incarnationally around my life
and leave them unwrapped while I
mistake the colorful tissues and bows
for the gifts within
and how,
within the baptismal gift of Christ's Body,
I prayerfully continue
to unwrap the question,
"What ought we to do?"

A CHRISTMAS NOTE

LUKE 2:1-14   "Suddenly there was with the
angel a multitude of the heavenly
host. . . ."

I met a little girl
one December evening
who stood as small
as a potted pine
with Christmas trees hiding
in the corners of her eyes.
"These many," as she held up three plump fingers
and smiled out loud.

Thomas R. Haney

"And what is this?" I asked
  with an enthusiasm
that more often frightens than reassures
  and she lowered her head
as shy as an unplayed grace note.

Inside the little black case
  she surrendered without fuss
  I discovered the smallest violin
  in the world
  wired for real sound
  as certainly as tiny fingers
are strung for counting happy birthdays.

  "Can you play this?" I asked in a softer tone
  She shook her head up and down
  as if it were a little round ball bouncing
  against a flat wooden paddle.

  "And whose birthday is next week?"
  I asked in a Christmas carol voice.
  She stood there as mute as her violin
  and all the notes yet to sound.

  "You know, Honey, tell him now,"
  her mother urged
  with unreserved maternal pride
"Baby Jesus," she answered coyly
  as though flirting with the words.

  "And do you have a birthday gift
  for Baby Jesus?" I asked.

216

TODAY'S SPIRITUALITY

Her eyes sparkled like reflecting tinsel.
   "Happy Birthday," she giggled softly.
"It's the recital . . . just a few notes,"
   her mother rushed to dispel
   any image of prodigy.
"I'm sure Baby Jesus will be very pleased
   when you play *Happy Birthday* for him,"
I said, and my words seemed to hug her
   comfortably.

Lord of the eternal Now
   and of a day of brith,
   of rustic stables
   and dusty carpenter shops,
   of foxes' dens and feathered nests,
Realtor for your Father's many mansions,
   make room for a little girl
   who wraps her squeaky notes
   with the tiny strings of her violin
   and slips her gift *pianissimo*
past gold and frankincense and myrrh.

Lord, give a Cana blessing to
   "just a few notes"
   until they fill the midnight sky
   with angels' song of glory and of peace,
   and bestow a lakeside blessing
   on those little fingers
   as they beckon all to worship
the infinite Note once made flesh.

Thomas R. Haney

A STORY OF CHRISTMAS BEAUTY

LUKE 2:1-7 "In those days Caesar Augustus
published a decree ordering a
census of the whole world."

In a far-off kingdom long ago
 a Princess was preparing once again
 to hate Christmas.
The royal hall would be gloriously transformed
 into shimmering decorations
 almost matching the magnificent star
 of that first Christmas jubilation.

The Princess would receive extravagant gifts
 beyond her ability to count.
But when Christmas was all over, the Princess
 would be what she always was: ugly.

In truth the Princess was not really ugly
 but plain-looking.
Yet each time she looked at herself in a mirror
 she would burst into a torrent of tears.
That is why one day she ordered all the mirrors
 in the castle to be covered forever.
Still each night she would recall the image
 she had seen of herself in the mirror
 and quietly sob herself to sleep.

TODAY'S SPIRITUALITY

It was at Christmas especially
  when all looked so beautiful
  that the plain-looking Princess
  would become so bleakly depressed
  that a shadow of sadness spread
throughout the whole castle and the entire kingdom,
  and Christmas became the saddest day of the
  year.

On this particular Christmas eve, however
  the plain-looking Princess' maiden aunt
  from a land far away
  came to spend Christmas at the castle
  and everyone but the Princess
  was overjoyed to see her.

The maiden aunt, knowing of her niece's plight,
  visited her in her dark brooding.
"I have come, my child," her aunt spoke cheerfully,
  "to bring you a gift not of jewels
nor of white stallions nor of finest silk nor of gold
  but a gift that is a secret — the secret
  of becoming truly beautiful."

The plain-looking Princess listened wide-eyed
  as her aunt revealed the secret
  of true beauty:
"First, to be beautiful, smile at everyone.
Secondly, always look for what is beautiful
  in people and in all God-given gifts.
Thirdly, do a kind deed for each person you meet."

Thomas R. Haney

The plain-looking Princess thought and thought.
That night instead of crying herself to sleep,
she prayed that the Christ Child would help her
to use the gift her aunt had given her.

On Christmas morning the plain-looking Princess
rose from her bed and going through
the castle from top to bottom
she smiled at each and every person
from the King to the smallest serf,
looked for beauty all around her
and performed kind deeds for everyone.

This she did the next day
and the day after that
and every day of her life until
each day was Christmas day.

And the word went forth throughout the kingdom
"We have the most beautiful Princess
in all the land
in the whole wide world."

SOMETIMES I WISH . . .

JOHN 6:60-69   "Lord, to whom shall we go?"

Mostly my knowledge of God
is like a spider web
slow, meticulous, thread

220

TODAY'S SPIRITUALITY

by anguished theological thread,
painfully transparent
and very, very delicate,
woven into a corner of an endless universe
    where the cracked plaster of my mind
    reveals my crawling search.

Sometimes I wish my knowledge
    of God was like a wave,
    not a tidal wave
    but the kind a surfer hangs
    a perfect ten on;
or like a flash of irrational
    magnetism that pulls
    two people who are nameless
    to one another
and snaps them together in electric curiosity.

Sometimes it's as simple as
    a question that already knows the answer.

With Peter I seek the truth hidden
    from the beginning in mystery,
"To whom shall we go?"
It's like asking, "Where's up?"
Especially since Up has come down
    and the Eternal Now is forever Future,
    luring us forward and upward.

"To whom shall we go?"
    and he tells us a story.

Thomas R. Haney

Once there was a man who made
   a journey to Jericho. . . .
and don't worry about what you'll
   eat on the journey
   because "I am the bread of life."

And so it dawns like
   the sun leap-frogging
   the distant mountain —
the essential knowledge is far more
   than a web of memorized theses.

It's splitting a cold beer with a friend
   on a hot summer afternoon
   and knowing that God has touched
   our world and made it holy.

It's hugging your wife in the kitchen
   with microwave awe,
or pounding the beat of a
   cobbled work routine,
or watching your favorite team
   crash into a last minute win
and knowing that God walked the harvest.

It's having sacred moments and sacred places
   so that every moment and every place
   will be experienced as holy.

Webless knowledge is the process
   of experiencing the Incarnate God
   in our carnal blessings

TODAY'S SPIRITUALITY

amid the lilies of the field
where foxes have their dens
and mustard seeds dream
of low housing for the winged messengers
of a grape-vine Providence.

A CUP SHARED

MARK 9:38-41   "Anyone who gives you a cup of
                    water . . . will surely not lose his
                    reward."

A man caked with desert sand
    as thick as mortar
    fell to his apparent dying
    as his parched throat closed
    as tight as a vise
when out of nowhere a hand lifted his head
    and forced a few drops of water
    into his imprisoned mouth
and the water, cool in its quenching power
    grew hot in the fervor
    of the stranded victim
    who vowed to be refreshing water
    in the deserts of others' lives.

A CUP OF WATER, COOL AND FRESH
    GIVEN IN HIS NAME
WILL NEVER LEAVE THE SHARERS
    EVER QUITE THE SAME.

Thomas R. Haney

"Master," the young disciple spoke
  with a respect as sincere
  as the fragrance of a rose,
"how can I grow in holiness and love?"

The master of spiritual insight
  picked up a crusty cup
  with a crack as obvious
  as the noonday sun.
"When you can give a full cup of water
  to quench another's thirst
  with this cup as it is now,
you will be holy and full of love."

  A CUP OF WATER, COOL AND FRESH
    GIVEN IN HIS NAME
  WILL NEVER LEAVE THE SHARERS
    EVER QUITE THE SAME.

When you sit dreaming dreams
  of some heroic deed
please remember the fleeting scene
  of a widow long ago
  and a living lesson still
who dropped two coins into the depths
  of everlasting commendation.
And ponder, if you will, the simple clue
  of the common cup
and the water offered to another's thirst.

TODAY'S SPIRITUALITY

A CUP OF WATER, COOL AND FRESH
  GIVEN IN HIS NAME
WILL NEVER LEAVE THE SHARERS
  EVER QUITE THE SAME.

When all the heroic stories of love are told,
  star-studded romance
  will seldom be the theme
  and oceans of passion will dry
  in the hollow phrases of description
and as these stories unfold in all their glory
  the tale will surely be told
  of those who thirsted
  and those who loved
  and of the transformation
celebrated over a cup of common water.

A CUP OF WATER, COOL AND FRESH
  GIVEN IN HIS NAME
WILL NEVER LEAVE THE SHARERS
  EVER QUITE THE SAME.

A POET'S SONG

MARK 8:27-35   ". . . who do you say that I am?"

No one knew him and few could care.
  He'd come from somewhere
  and would no doubt leave one day.

225

Thomas R. Haney

For now all they longed for was his stories
   that they could hold stars
   in the palms of their hands
   and feel rainbows rub
   gently against their cheeks
and at the end of each story day he would softly
   sing:

   AND IF YOU SHOULD EVER TELL MY
   STORY
      TELL IT PLEASE THIS WAY:
   I STROVE WITH ALL CREATIVE MIGHT
      'TIL I COULD NO LONGER STAY.

   AND IF MY STORIES DRAW YOU NEAR
      SING A HEARTFELT PRAYER WITH ME
   FOR STORIES HAVE A MAGIC POWER
      ONLY HEARTS CAN HEAR AND SEE.

One day as he walked through mist
   as lavish as a willow's tears
   he told a tale of a dreamy poet
   who strolled to the ocean's edge
   and gazed forlornly at the distance
   of the golden sunset as it slipped
   into the hungry waves' gray mouth.
I will go out there, he thought, and push the colors
   high
   a glorious banner for ceaseless salute
   near as seagulls sailing ocean spray.

TODAY'S SPIRITUALITY

A lovely maiden happened by and, as though
   reading the young poet's mind,
   spoke gently as an evening breeze,
"Let the sunset go, dear heart, and it surely
   will return again
   for that is the way of colors —
   the more you let go, the more
   they bring the greatest joy.
It's the way of life and the way of love.
   You may anticipate only
   that which you let go."

It was the end of the story and the end of the day
   so he began softly to sing:

   AND IF YOU SHOULD EVER TELL MY
   STORY
      TELL IT PLEASE THIS WAY:
   I STROVE WITH ALL CREATIVE MIGHT
      'TIL I COULD NO LONGER STAY.

   AND IF MY STORIES DRAW YOU NEAR
      SING A HEARTFELT PRAYER WITH ME
   FOR STORIES HAVE A MAGIC POWER
      ONLY HEARTS CAN HEAR AND SEE.

No one ever really knew his name
   but everyone knew his stories
   and long, long after he had left them
   they told his stories time and again
and through his stories came to know him well
   and celebrated the song he had sung:

Thomas R. Haney

AND IF YOU SHOULD EVER TELL MY
STORY
   TELL IT PLEASE THIS WAY:
I STROVE WITH ALL CREATIVE MIGHT
   'TIL I COULD NO LONGER STAY.

AND IF MY STORIES DRAW YOU NEAR
   SING A HEARTFELT PRAYER WITH ME
FOR STORIES HAVE A MAGIC POWER
   ONLY HEARTS CAN HEAR AND SEE.